TENACIOUS: A CHAMPIONSHIP MENTALITY FOR YOUNG ATHLETES

THE 15-STEP GUIDE TO PERFORM YOUR BEST, AND BE COMPETITIVELY GREAT WHEN YOUR BEST PERFORMANCE IS REQUIRED

MIKE HOGAN

CONTENTS

INTRODUCTION

66 *The ideal attitude is to be physically loose and mentally tight.*

— ARTHUR ASHE (TENNIS GREAT)

What does it take to become a truly great athlete? Is it simply a matter of talent or is it all about hard work? Is it luck that helps someone achieve "greatness" or does their network come into play? For a young athlete who is working to improve their game and chase after their dreams, these are all valid questions to ask. The thing is, though, being a champion isn't just about talent, hard work, luck, or connections. Doubtless, some of these things do come into play from time to time and can help an athlete along the way to stardom. But in reality, the mark of a truly great athlete is something very different: It's simply a matter of how tenacious they are.

Tenacity is vital for achieving anything in life, whether it's becoming the great athlete you know you can be or a rising star in the business world. Don't believe me? Take a look at the stories of professional climber Emily Harrington, and the unstoppable businesswoman, Sarah Blakeley. Emily Harrington is the first woman to ever climb the terrifyingly difficult Golden Gate route found on the El Capitan mountain, a feat that very few climbers to date have achieved. The thing is, Harrington didn't manage to get to the top of this route on her first try. Instead, she fell about 50 feet, banged her (luckily helmeted) head against a ledge, and suffered a concussion. Then, once she was all better, she came back and tried again, despite how terrified she was of falling.

(Pompliano, 2021). She climbed the route once more, despite her fear, and this time she managed to conquer it.

Sarah Blakeley, the youngest ever self-made billionaire, has a very similar story. When she first started out, she wanted to be an attorney, which meant she had to pass the LSATs to get into law school. She failed quite spectacularly at this. Then, she went on to audition to play Goofy—yes, the cartoon character—at Disney World and failed to get the part because she was too short. About a year after that, she ended up moving in with her mom. Now, does that sound like a success story to you?

Blakeley didn't allow her failures to keep her down, though. Instead, she ended up creating the first-ever Spanx (which is a kind of undergarment, if you're unfamiliar with it) while getting ready for a party, no less. Then, she took her Spanx idea and ran with it, turning it into a multi-billion-dollar business venture. Blakeley had to use all of her savings to do this—all $5,000 of them—but this was a risk she was willing to take, and one that clearly paid off.

Harrington and Blakeley's stories have two commonalities, as you'll notice: Both of these individuals experienced failures of staggering proportions on their way to ultimate success, and neither of them let their previous failures (or their fear, for that matter) keep them from going after the things they wanted.

That, right there, is what tenacity is. Tenacity is the thing that allows you to keep moving forward, even after you face failure and rejection. It's the thing that keeps you from caving in to your fears, whatever form they may take. It's the reason why Harrington and Blakeley were able to achieve their dreams, and it's why a young athlete such as yourself can do so as well.

Another term for tenacity is "mental toughness," and it's an absolutely crucial ingredient to have if you want to be successful in your chosen field. At least, that's what all the professional coaches and athletes out there believe. This is because mental toughness can keep you from being shaken up by the obstacles, setbacks, and failures you might face as you fight to achieve your dreams (Gutierrez, 2015).

The problem is, mental toughness is something a lot of people, especially young, budding athletes struggle to gain. This is understandable, as developing mental toughness can be really hard when you're struggling with a pessimistic mindset, say, or you're afraid of disappointing others, such as your coach, teammates, even your parents. Many young athletes grapple with feelings of inadequacy and negative thoughts, they believe that success is dependent on the ability to network and even luck. If you keep training according to old-school (and thus, out of date) trends, and have no idea how to express the goals you want to achieve, you will struggle to succeed.

While these obstacles are all understandable and to be expected, they're not insurmountable. Mental toughness isn't something you're born with or without, after all. Instead, it's something that you can achieve by putting in the work and following the right kind of guidance. The thing is, great athletes don't just appear out of the blue. They start out with some degree of skill that they improve upon with the right kind of training, and with the help of the right mentor.

Think about it for a minute: Do you believe Luke Skywalker could have achieved all that he did without Obi-Wan Kenobi and Yoda's guidance? Would Spider-Man be who he is without his uncle, Ben Parker? Of course not. These heroes needed those guiding figures so they could develop their skills, find their moral compasses, and choose the directions that they wanted to go in. They needed the strength and support of their mentors as they grew and learned from their mistakes and increased their mental toughness, just like any young athlete looking to advance and improve.

As a former college and professional athlete and the father of three young athletes myself, this is something that I'm intimately familiar with. I've both seen and experienced how vital a good mentor can be in helping to increase an athlete's tenacity. I've also seen and experienced how difficult bolstering your tenacity can be when you don't know how to go about it. This, of course, is where *Tenacious* comes in. The unfortunate truth is, finding the right mentor for you can take a little time. It might also take some trial and effort. But that doesn't mean you should lose valuable time that you can use to strengthen your mentality. Hence, my writing of this book.

What I mean to achieve in *Tenacious*, then, is to provide young athletes like yourself with the tools and knowledge that you need to cultivate a strong mindset, which is the very cornerstone of becoming a champion and a force to be reckoned with. It's to show you how you can achieve this mindset, no matter where you are in your athletic journey, so long as you put in the time and effort. It's to demonstrate how you can use what you learn to grow from your failures and mistakes, and anytime you stumble and fall, get back on your feet stronger than before.

The simple fact of the matter is, you're more than capable of achieving all this and more. The roots of tenacity and the spirit of a champion already live in you. You just need to know how to pull them out, bring them to the surface, and fortify them. Once you do, you'll be surprised to see just how far you go in your chosen athletic field and just how many obstacles (that maybe seemed insurmountable to you in the past) you can overcome, so long as you try.

PART I

AN ODE TO MENTAL TOUGHNESS

1

TOUGHNESS EQUALS PUNISHMENT

You can have anything you want, if you're willing to give up the belief that you can't have it.

— DR. ROBERT ANTHONY

Before we can begin to explore how you can use mental toughness or tenacity to achieve your athletic dreams, we must first understand what it is. Tenacity is, unfortunately, as misunderstood a concept as it is an important one. This is because a lot of people confuse tenacity for punishment. In doing so, they take the saying, "no pain, no gain" in an entirely different way than it's intended. Since using a tool—and tenacity can be thought of as a tool—that they don't understand isn't easy, they often fail to achieve the results that they want. Obviously, this is something that you want to avoid and you can only do so by grasping the true meaning of tenacity.

UNDERSTANDING MENTAL TOUGHNESS

Tenacity can be defined as the process you use to develop your ability to do your best work and give your best performance (in whatever field you're in), no matter how hard the conditions you're facing are and what obstacles you go up against. It's your ability to keep going no matter how harsh things get without losing your hope, resilience, and optimism.

A lot of athletes, coaches, and even sports psychologists —yes, that is a profession—consider mental toughness to be a psychological edge for athletes (*What is mental toughness?*, n.d.). This is because mental toughness has several characteristics that you can use in a game or a match.

The first of these characteristics is a winner's mindset. Having a winner's mindset means having the attitude of a champion. It means having an unwavering belief in yourself, your talent, and your abilities. Another characteristic that mental toughness endows you with is "hyper-focus," which allows you to focus on your goals without being distracted by anything else, such as the cheering or booing of the courtside fans, for instance.

One of the greatest characteristics of a winner's mindset is that it makes it easier for you to manage your stress. Athletes understandably experience a great deal of stress, anxiety, and fear when they go out to play a game or match. A mentally tough athlete, though, is able to manage these things without caving in to them. More than managing them, such an athlete can even use them. This is because stress isn't supposed to be the debilitating thing that a lot of us make it out to be.

Stress is part of our natural survival instinct. Eons ago, we used to get stressed when we were under threat, like from a predator, for example, and had to run away. The stress we felt would get adrenaline pumping through our bodies. It would also get more oxygen to our legs and both of these things would allow us to run away faster. While we no longer live in close proximity to predators, at least most of the time, our stress reaction still accomplishes these exact same things. That means that by learning to manage our stress, we can use the changes it causes in our bodies—the adrenaline and oxygen spikes—to our advantage and move faster and be stronger in a game. This only works, though, if we are able to manage our stress. Hence, the importance of mental toughness.

In keeping with that, tenacity also allows you to push your limits when you need to. You know those moments when you have to score one final point to win, and you're suddenly able to run faster than you ever have before? That's what pushing your limits means and that is what you will be able to do when you increase your mental toughness.

Of course, you also increase your ability to fail well. What does that mean? Well, remember Emily Harrington and Sarah Blakeley's stories about how they faced epic failures and then got back to their feet and tried again? That's what "failing well" means. It also means learning important lessons from your failures by asking yourself "What could I have done better?" and then actually doing those things in the future. As an athlete, failure is something you're going to experience at least some of the time, no matter how talented or hard working you are. Given that, learning to fail well is essential if you want to be a champion in the making.

A final characteristic of mental toughness is that it prepares you for future games, matches, and challenges. This is something that can enable you to use your past experiences—both your successes and your failures—to predict how future plays may unfold, and devise strategies to counter them. It's something that can keep you from being taken aback, and help you recover quickly from unexpected failures, mistakes, and obstacles.

Looking at all these different characteristics, it's easy to see how important mental toughness is in sports. Yet, despite this, it's a relatively new concept in the sports world. The term "mental toughness" was first used in sports in the 1980s by psychologist Jim Loeher and football coach Vince Lombardi. Since then, it has evolved into a field of study that looks into how elite athletes can perform better. This field of study has yielded numerous training techniques, strategies, and tactics that both professional sportsmen and budding ones can take advantage of.

The more they studied mental toughness as a psychological tool, the more people came to realize just how many advantages it has to offer. It was discovered, for example, that mental toughness helps people manage their stress, as you know. This reduces the likelihood that people who practice mental toughness will experience mental health problems, which can be caused by high levels of chronic stress and anxiety (*Why mental toughness*, 2020). Of course, this situation also has to do with how mental toughness increases positive behavior and positive thoughts. After all, being resilient or optimistic isn't easy if your mind is crowded with overwhelmingly negative thoughts.

Another major benefit of mental toughness is that it increases your performance, as you may have gathered by now. If you're wondering just how much of a difference it can make in this regard, mental toughness is known to increase performance by as much as 25% (*Why mental toughness*, 2020). This can be attributed to the fact that people who are mentally tough are usually more competitive and have a greater sense of purpose than opponents and even teammates who aren't quite as tenacious. Michael Jordan, for instance, is a great example of this, seeing as he always went out to games with the intent of winning and being the best.

What's one unexpected advantage of tenacity? It's that it can actually make you more open to learning. This makes sense when you think about it. Tenacious people —be they athletes or not—don't operate under the belief that they're perfect, even when they fully believe that they're the best. Instead, they recognize that they can always improve their game. What's more, they understand that they should *work* to improve their game. To that end, they keep training, learning new strategies, and developing new techniques.

This is why a great football team would study their opponent's previous games, for instance. They'd know that in doing so, they would be able to understand their opponent's strategies better and develop counter strategies for them. Tenacity makes players more able to learn from their own mistakes and failures, too. Put simply, people who are mentally tough are both able and willing to learn new things and show growth.

Being able to learn from your mistakes and failures requires showing a degree of resilience. Luckily, resilience is still one more benefit that mental toughness can endow you with. Resilience can help you overcome various difficulties, but that's not all it's good for. At the same time, it can raise the level of confidence you have in yourself and your abilities, which translates into you performing even better in the field (Morin, 2016). Which athlete wouldn't want that, honestly?

Finally, all of this can make an athlete a great deal more ambitious. Ambition and a desire to win are key to becoming a champion. Your confidence in your abilities, your high level of performance, and your commitment to your game are all things that can fuel your ambition. They're things that can feed your desire to win whatever championship or race you're part of. They can help you to set the goals that will become the steps you need to take on your way to being crowned the king or queen of whatever court you're on.

The Importance of Mental Toughness for an Athlete

Clearly, mental toughness has a vast array of benefits and advantages to offer to any athlete at any point in their career. But why is it so important, so crucial, that athletes develop their mental toughness? Why does mental toughness matter so much in the context of a single game, a championship, or even an athlete's career? Mental toughness is vital in the context of these things for three specific reasons:

1. It allows an athlete to develop a winning mentality.
2. It builds that athlete's character and promotes stability.
3. It gives that athlete the courage they need to challenge the status quo.

What do those things mean, exactly? Well, let's scrutinize that by taking a look at what a "winning mentality" is. Your mentality is the mindset you go into a game with. Think about it like this: If you go into a match with all these negative thoughts running through your head, then odds are, you're not going to be able to perform your best. If you go into it with thoughts that aren't in any way related to your match pulsing through your mind, then you probably aren't going to be able to focus on the game all that well. If you go into it with neutral thoughts, where you're not pumping yourself up but aren't actively putting yourself down, either—in other words with a mediocre mindset—then, again, you're not going to be able to perform at your best (Mariama-Arthur, 2016).

If you go into it with thoughts of winning, though? If you go into it fully believing in your abilities, completely focused on the game that you're going to play and having absolute faith that you're about to perform your best? Well, then your body and mind will respond to those thoughts. The winning mentality that you put yourself into will help you perform in a way that reflects that and win your game or match.

What about character growth and stability? Can mental toughness really promote character growth, seeing as you're not a character in a novel or a movie? The short answer to that question is a resounding "yes." As for the how… The thing about mental toughness is that it gives an athlete grit. In sport psychology, grit is considered to be an athlete's ability to thrive under adversity (Mariama-Arthur, 2016). According to research, grit is something that increases people's stamina. The higher someone's stamina is, the faster they'll be able to run, the higher they'll be able to jump, the harder they'll be able to hit or kick a ball, and the longer they'll be able to keep going. It can be said, then, that grit is just as important for an athlete as, say, intelligence, meaning they're able to strategize and use their problem-solving skills mid-game or match.

So, what does grit have to do with character growth? Everything. The thing about growth is that it cannot happen when a person remains stagnant or stuck. Overcoming adversity—meaning the challenges and obstacles we face—is something that forces us to use all our creativity, abilities, and problem-solving skills. Like muscles, these are things that develop more as we use them. So, when we have grit, we expand on all these things and more. In expanding on them, we can over-come our obstacles. As we do so, we become more aware of our strengths, our weaknesses, and how we can improve upon them. In other words, we undergo growth.

As for stability... The reason mental toughness affords athletes stability is that it gives them a set goal to work toward. When you have a set goal to strive for, you essentially have a reason to keep going, despite how many struggles you might face. This reason can be a remarkable thing to hold onto to keep you from waver-ing. It can keep your confidence levels up, even in the face of loss. It can put you on your path, going straight as an arrow. In other words, it can ensure that you remain *stable*.

Last, but not least, tenacity allows you to challenge the status quo. The status quo in the world of sports means the existing practices, techniques, strategies, training methods, and the like that are already in place. As important as such things are, they're in a state of constant flux, or at least, they should be. Otherwise, the game cannot evolve or reach new heights.

Developing new techniques and advancing them are responsibilities that largely fall on the shoulders of athletes. They're the ones that keep working on their moves, coming up with new ones (or new iterations of old moves), and then perfecting them. Take David Beckham as an example of this.

Beckham is known for his Bending Free Kick, as you may know. This move is one of his signatures, it essentially puts a curve in the arc of the ball when he kicks it, making it near impossible to catch (Quashie, 2016). Beckham could not have perfected this shot, though, had he not worked on it and disregarded the naysayers who believed he should just stick to perfecting the shots that everyone else used. Neither could Michal Jordan have perfected his fadeaway if he had listened to others and given in to the status quo.

Challenging the status quo is something that takes courage. It's hard to do what you think is right, after all, if all the others around you are insisting that you're wrong. But courage is essential in any sport and not just for challenging the status quo. It's also a necessary ingredient for facing your fears, the way Emily

Harrington did, for example. Face whatever challenges are in your way and become the champion, even the leader that you want to be.

What You Must Remember

Becoming a champion, however, isn't exactly an easy thing to achieve, no matter how tenacious you are. It takes a lot of hard work and dedication, which is something you need to be prepared for if you want to chase after this dream. Being a talented tennis player, wrestler, or any other kind of athlete will never be enough to win the medals and championships you want. Not unless you're willing to put a great deal of effort into fighting for what you want. The fight can be difficult from time to time, of course, but that's a good thing. After all, would you really want that title or cup if it was something that could be gotten easily, and by anyone, at that?

Just because becoming a champion means walking a tough road doesn't mean it should be devoid of fun. Let's say you're a basketball player and a very talented one at that. Let's also say you actually don't like playing basketball. If that is the case, you're not going to be having any fun out on the court. In fact, you're probably going to be miserable, wishing that the game was over already. Your heart, as they say, won't be in the game, in this case, which is hardly conducive to winning. The fact is, not liking the game you're playing can not only make you miserable, but it'll likely keep you from winning as well. Because—how can you win a game, if you don't even enjoy what you're doing?

The first two things you need to know when going into the world of sports, then, are that sports should actually be fun, and that becoming a champion takes a great deal of effort, but it's worth it. Another thing you absolutely should know is that failures will be a part of your journey along the way. There's not a single athlete out there, dead or alive, who hasn't experienced failure at some point or another, and this includes the greats. Serena Williams, Muhammed Ali, Michael Jordan, Michael Phelps, Usain Bolt, Florence Griffith Joyner, Pelé, Marta Vieria da Silva… They have all experienced failure and loss at some point in their lives. Want to know what made them different from their peers? They learned from those failures and grew from them. They didn't let failure keep them down, and any athlete that wants to become a champion needs to do the same.

Another thing that makes great athletes different is that they recognize that their worth doesn't count on their performance. A bad game, match, or practice doesn't automatically make you a bad player. In fact, it's expected for you to have a bad day or three every now and again.

This is where something known as the rule of thirds comes in, at least according to Olympic athlete Alexi Pappas. Pappas says that when you're chasing a goal—like winning Olympic gold as a long distance runner—you'll feel really good at a third of your practices, games, and matches. You'll feel mediocre in another third and crappy in the last third (Swenson, 2021). That's normal and it's something that athletes have come to expect. So, if you feel that you've underperformed at a game or practice, you shouldn't take that as a sign that you're not a good athlete. Instead, you should learn what you can from it by asking yourself "What could I have done better or differently?" You should also understand that that day was just a regular part of "the rule of thirds," and move on. In other words, you should remember to take the pressure off of yourself a little bit, so you can keep moving forward and improving.

A last note to make is that you need to respect your opponents and act respectfully toward them. It's normal to get heated during a match or a game, but that doesn't mean you should be intentionally belligerent, aggressive, or hurtful toward your opponents, even if you consider them to be your rivals. Instead, you should afford them the respect that they're owed, just as you should be shown respect by them. In other words, you should value sportsmanship and sportsmanship-like conduct at all times, both on the court and off of it.

2

FACING YOUR VILLAINS

The brave man isn't he who doesn't feel afraid, but he who conquers that fear.

— NELSON MANDELA

Fear is one of the most basic emotions you can feel. It's something we all experience from time to time, and it's perfectly normal. Yet, despite this, there's this erroneous idea that a brave athlete or a courageous person is someone who doesn't feel fear. This is patently untrue.

Fear is a very strong emotion, one that doesn't come with an off switch. You can't stop yourself from feeling fear any more than you can stop yourself from feeling hungry or getting thirsty, because fear is a part of you. That doesn't mean, however, that fear has to be debilitating for you. It doesn't mean that it has to keep you from going after your dreams, achieving them, or performing at your best. True, fear can do all of that, but only if you let it, because you may not be able to control fear, but you certainly can control how you react to it. The mark of a brave athlete, then, isn't that they can stop themselves from being afraid. It's that they do the things that they're afraid—sometimes even terrified of.

If that's the case, how can you overcome your fears? How can you make it so that they never hold you back ever again? To be able to do this, you'll first have to understand what you're afraid of. You'll have to name your fears, because, let's face it, the unnamed monsters lurking in the dark are always scarier than the ones that you can see, name, and fight against.

THE WORST FEARS OF AN ATHLETE

"What am I afraid of?" This is one of the first questions you have to ask yourself when you set out to become a great athlete. When you think about it, there are a great many things athletes might be afraid of, and no, I don't mean things like spiders or snakes, unless one happens to wander into the court you're on, of course. The fears that a typical athlete has to face tend to be a little more psychological and a little less concrete than that, which is part of what makes them hard to face.

These are fears that you might have at any point in your athletic career. You can face some in your rookie years and others when you become a pro. You can go for years thinking you've conquered a fear before it suddenly makes a resurgence. Given that, you need to understand what your fears are, because only by doing so can you begin facing them.

On the whole, an athlete's fears will fall into one of seven categories. These categories are:

1. Limiting beliefs
2. Low or fragile self-confidence

3. Breakdowns in trust
4. High expectations
5. Fear of failure
6. Perfectionism
7. Sports anxiety

Limiting Beliefs

Some of those terms probably sound unfamiliar to you. Others, you might have heard of. Whatever the case may be, let's take a closer look at each of these different types of fears so that we can start figuring out how to confront them, starting with limiting beliefs.

Limiting beliefs are beliefs you have about yourself that limit your thinking, ability to perform, or even willingness to pick up a sport that you're interested in. In other words, they're beliefs that you have that might hold you back from going after the things you want and pursuing your goals and passions (Manson, 2020).

Limiting beliefs can pertain to any number of things. They may be related to age, for instance, in that they can cause an athlete to fear they're too old or too young to try out a new move or even get into some kind of sport. They may be related to their personal traits, making them conclude that they're too dumb to do something or too weak to even try. Interestingly enough, limiting beliefs can also apply to your own feelings. You might conclude, for instance, that you're too stressed, embarrassed, anxious, or *"insert feeling here"* to give something a try.

As you can see, all of these beliefs have to do with yourself and your abilities. But limiting beliefs don't have to be about you, exclusively. They might also be about the world or even about life. Limiting beliefs about the world pertain to the things that we believe others will allow us to do or not to do. A great example of this is the fear of disappointing others. If you are a basketball player and you want to become a baseball player instead (the way Michael Jordan did for a period of time), your fear that this will disappoint your fans (or your parents, who, let's say, are basketball players themselves) might keep you from making the switch.

Another example of limiting beliefs about the world is the fear of facing prejudice. Let's say that you're a quarterback and a really great one at that. You mean to play in the NFL, but you're hesitant because you're black and most quarterbacks are white, for some reason. This situation can make you hesitant to try out for quarterback, in case you end up facing racial prejudice.

Similarly, if you're a woman, you might hold yourself back from signing up for team sports, because so many people still consider sports to be a man's domain. These limiting beliefs are common despite the fact that we live in an era where great athletes such as Serena Williams exist, and great teams exist like the US women's national soccer team, which has won four World Cup Titles and four Olympic gold medals to date (Goal, 2021).

Believing that you're special, too special for the world to handle, is one very unexpected limiting belief about the world (Manson, 2020). There's another word for this kind of belief: entitlement. Entitlement is something that many people with talent, not just athletes, have. Such people often end up not using their talents, and thus, don't get to improve on them. They also don't get to go after the things they really want, like becoming a great athlete of the caliber that they've already deluded themselves into thinking they are.

What about the fear of having missed the boat? You might face another limiting belief that you missed your shot to become a great athlete and there's nothing you can do about it now, so you don't even try. Another such belief is that you simply don't have enough time on your hands to go after your athletic dreams. This is similar to that excuse some people give about not having enough time to hit the gym or work out a couple of times a week for the sake of their health. In both cases, these excuses can keep the individual in question from even trying to work out.

The key to overcoming limiting beliefs is to work on changing your mentality, as that's where they stem from. This requires putting in the work you'll need to switch from a negative mindset to a positive one through things like positive self-talk. You'll learn how to do that in the coming chapters.

Low or Fragile Self-Confidence

So, those are limiting beliefs. What about self-confidence, then? How might your level of self-confidence become a source of struggle for you on your way to achieving your dreams? Your self-confidence is, essentially, how much you believe in your athletic abilities and your ability to perform in a game or a match (Heistand, 2021). In other words, it's how much you believe in yourself in general and how much you believe in yourself right before or during a specific match, competition, race, or game.

Lacking self-confidence, or losing your self-confidence easily when you make a slight mistake during a game, for instance, can have drastic consequences for an athlete. For one thing, it can easily keep them from performing their best. For another, it can keep them from performing certain moves or strategies because they feel they can't do them well, and this can, in turn, cost them the victory. An athlete can feel perfectly confident during practices and while training, but can sometimes lose it when they have to perform. This can become a huge source of pressure for them, which, again, will prove to be a massive hindrance.

Luckily, low or fragile self-confidence isn't something that's impossible to recover from. There are numerous things you can do to increase and fortify your self-confidence. The first step to fixing low self-confidence is recognizing the signs. The second step is remembering that you're not the only individual to experience this. Plenty of athletes, rookies, and pros alike struggle with their self-confidence from time to time and, yes, that includes the so-called greats. Low self-confidence is a universal struggle, one that athletes and non-athletes all face. When you recognize all these as facts, you are able to take at least some of the pressure off of yourself. You're also able to nullify some of your self-blame, self-anger, self-criticism, and heavy thoughts like "Why am I like this?" As an added bonus, you get to feel just a little less alone, which makes dealing with your self-confidence a bit easier to do.

How exactly do you do that? By focusing on positive thoughts, constructive feedback, and self-encouragement, all of which you'll learn to use properly in due time. For now, the main thing you should remember is that by focusing on and using these things, you can improve your mindset, increase your self-confidence, and in the process, increase your mental toughness.

The other thing you should know is that you won't be able to do all of this in the span of a single day. If you were to go to the gym, you wouldn't be able to see immediate progress in the form of weight loss and toned muscles. Instead, you'd see gradual improvements until one day you woke up to realize you had lost a lot of weight and gained a lot of muscle tone. The same logic applies to self-confidence and how it's developed. Odds are, you won't go from being someone who struggles with lack of self-confidence to being the most confident person in the world. However, you'll be able to do so, bit by bit, over time.

Breakdown in Trust

What about trust? What does trust have to do with fear? Well, when you become an athlete, you have to put your trust in three different things: yourself, your teammates (if you have them), and your coach or trainer. If you don't trust yourself and your abilities, you won't be able to use them properly. As such, you won't be able to perform as well as you otherwise would. If you don't trust your teammates, on the other hand, you won't be able to rely on them during a game. Take basketball as an example. Who would be more likely to win a game in basketball: a player who trusts his teammates to have his back and keeps passing the ball to them, thereby making it hard for his opponent to steal it? Or one who holds onto the ball and refuses to pass if he can avoid it, making it easier for his opponent to block his shots and steal the ball in the process?

How about your coach? Why is it problematic for you to fear trusting them? Well, your coach's job is to prepare you for future games. It's to develop effective strategies, counter strategies, and tactics for you and your teammates to use when you're going up against your opponents. It's to help you improve your own techniques, spot your areas of improvement, and help you work on them. If you don't trust your coach to do these things for you, and do them well, then you won't be able to fight effectively against your opponents. You also won't be able to see what your weaknesses are, and thus, won't be able to improve upon them.

Now, there are several reasons why you might be afraid of trusting your teammates and even your coach. One of these is overthinking (Janssen, 2016). In sports psychology this is alternatively known as "jamming" and it can effectively paralyze you mid-game. This can easily cost you valuable opportunities to score. It can also prevent you from executing a strategy, be it defensive or offensive. Jamming can even cost you time, which is horrifying given the fact that in a match or a game, even a millisecond can mean the difference between victory and defeat.

Your trust issues can also keep you from trusting that your teammates will cover certain opponents, resulting in you over-focusing or becoming overly conscious of a specific target or opponent. This is known as "aiming" and can cause you to become blind to other things in the court that you really should be aware of. It can keep you from relying on your teammates, putting more pressure on you in the process, and thus, lowering your ability to perform.

A final way that your trust issues might manifest is called "forcing." Forcing is the official term for trying too hard to get a very specific outcome in a game or match. If you're too focused on hitting a home run, for instance, you might miss out on other strategies and techniques that require you to trust your teammates. Missing out on these techniques can cost you time, opportunities, and points that could have carried you to an easy victory if only you had let them.

High Expectations

In general, there's absolutely nothing wrong with being ambitious. Most athletes who want to get to a certain level of performance set themselves various goals. But the thing is, there's a big difference between goals and expectations. Your goals are the things you want to achieve in the short or long term. They're your motivators and the things that you work toward. Expectations, on the other hand, are rigid, unbendable statements that you make and they can put a lot of pressure on you. These are statements that usually begin with things like "I have to..." or "I need to..." (Cohn, n.d.).

Statements like these are problematic because they're inflexible. Their very rigidity makes them hard to meet, and when athletes fail to meet high expectations, they quickly become disheartened and even prone to giving up. An athlete who has high expectations might fear their inability to meet them, and this fear can keep them from trying their best. What all this means is that high expectations can negatively impact an athlete's performance in two very distinctive ways. This is why it's important that athletes set realistic goals for themselves instead of imposing expectations.

What's a realistic goal? A realistic goal—this will be covered in greater detail later on—is a measurable, specific, and flexible goal that you work to meet. It's something that you mean to achieve and that can be realistically achieved. It's a specific, easy to see target you set for yourself that, far from disheartening you, can motivate you, keep you going, and even fire you up when you need it to.

Fear of Failure

One of the most debilitating fears any athlete can face is the fear of failure. This is the kind of fear that makes you think things like, "What if I can't do it?" or "What if I'm not good enough?" The danger with this kind of thinking is that it can lead to the answer, "Well, if I'm not good enough, maybe I shouldn't even try," or "Why would I even bother, if I'm not going to be able to do it, anyway?"

Aside from keeping you from playing a game or even learning a sport, fear of failure can prevent you from taking a risk in a game or match. Yet, risk is essential to winning a victory in sports. Think about it, anytime you pass the ball in a team sport, like soccer, basketball, or football, you're taking a risk (Pottratz, 2013). By passing the ball, you're giving your opponent the opportunity to steal it if they move fast enough. But if you don't pass the ball, you won't be able to play efficiently or effectively. You probably won't be able to score any points either.

Given that, athletes have to take at least some kind of risk when they're in a match, race, or game. An athlete who has a fear of failure, though, can't do that. As a result, they'll end up playing it safe when they shouldn't. At best, this will result in their being unable to score. At worst, it will keep them (and their team) from doing their best and cost them the entire game.

To overcome your fear of failure, you first have to acknowledge that it's there. You cannot defeat this monster, after all, if you can't even see it. Once you do, the way to overcome your fear is to work on your self-confidence and the trust you have in your teammates.

Combined, these two things can allow you to leap over your fear, however strong it may be, and achieve feats you didn't think were possible.

Perfectionism

A lot of people, both athletes and non-athletes alike, think that perfectionism is a good thing. Unfortunately, they couldn't be more wrong. Perfectionism is this idea that you have to execute every move and strategy perfectly. In theory, this sounds like a good idea. The problem with it is simple, though: Perfect doesn't exist.

No matter how hard you train and how much you try, you'll never achieve perfection. A lot of athletes don't understand this fact. As a result, they keep chasing after perfection and they end up feeling like failures when they are naturally unable to do so. They see their inability to achieve perfection as some kind of personal failing, when it really, truly isn't. At best, this perception causes them to get angry and frustrated with themselves. At worst, it causes them to contemplate giving up. Thoughts like, "I'm never going to be able to get this right" start flooding their minds. Such thoughts understandably lead to a great deal of stress, anxiety, and even depression, none of which sound like the key ingredients that make for a champion (Sigl, n.d.).

Another problematic feature of perfectionism is that it often causes athletes to push themselves way too hard. In their desire to do things perfectly, they overwork themselves both physically and mentally. This obviously lowers their performance levels. It also runs the risk of causing them to burn out while giving their self-confidence a sound beating and messing with their ability to focus on the game.

Clearly, an athlete who wants to become a champion has to start moving away from perfection. But if you're not supposed to focus on being perfect, what are you supposed to focus on? The short answer: You're supposed to focus on doing your best. Doing your best isn't the same thing as doing perfectly. Not even close, because your best is a constantly moving target.

Let's say you're hitting the gym and working out. When you first started, you were able to do 30 push-ups. Now you're able to do 50, meaning you've shown a marked improvement. Back when you first started out, your best was 30 push-ups. Now, your new best is 50. What will your best be in the future, then? You'll have to keep practicing, setting motivating goals for yourself, and pushing forward to find that out.

Sports Anxiety

I'm sure you've heard of the term "stage fright" before. It's likely something that's familiar to someone who is into theater or a class president who has to give a speech before the entire school. Well, sports anxiety can essentially be considered a version of stage fright, except, you know, for athletes. Sports anxiety is the fear you feel during a game. You fear making a mistake that'll cost you or your team your shot at victory. You fear that you might be unable to perform as well as you otherwise could, which is the sports version of forgetting your lines. You fear choking at a crucial moment and thus being responsible for losing the game.

Sports anxiety can be a very intense feeling and it can quickly overtake you if you let it. Luckily, it's one fear that can be overcome by using the right strategies and coping mechanisms. This is something many professional athletes know on a deeply personal level, because, while going through sports anxiety can make you feel isolated, it's actually a very common phenomenon. Scientists believe between 30–60% of all athletes have experienced sports anxiety at one point or another (Swaim, 2022). Yes, that includes the pros.

Sports anxiety can present with both physical and mental symptoms. If you want to deal with your sports anxiety, you must first be able to recognize it. Only then will you know to turn to your coping mechanisms, after all. In keeping with that, these are the physical symptoms you'll need to be on the lookout for:

- a racing heartbeat, which pumps hormones like cortisol and adrenaline through your veins
- tremors in your limbs and sometimes throughout your body, as a result of all that adrenaline
- tense muscles and possibly a headache, if you're gritting your teeth
- hyperventilation, feeling like you're unable to catch your breath
- digestion issues, seeing as your body, which has gone into fight or flight mode, will start diverting blood away from non-essential systems (like your digestion system) to your limbs, so you can run and fight harder, making it difficult for you to actually process and keep food down

There are also some mental symptoms that come with sports anxiety, as you know:

- an inability to focus on your game
- worry about how others are judging your performance
- anxiety, overthinking and forgetting moves you usually perform on reflex
- lower levels of self-confidence than usual

If you recognize one or more of these signs, you need to turn to your coping strategies immediately. Most coping strategies that deal with sports anxiety are stress-management techniques. Calming breathing exercises are a good example. So is meditating for 5–10 minutes, if you're able to. Talking to your fellow teammates (if you have them) or your coach can also prove helpful. If your sports anxiety is really bad, then talking to a trained professional, meaning a therapist who specializes in sports anxiety or performance anxiety in general is a good idea.

Additional Fears

The typical fears that an athlete will have to face and overcome can sometimes be made worse by additional, smaller anxieties and fears. These exacerbate certain aspects of things an athlete might be feeling and think-ing, making overcoming their fear all the more difficult. These more minor fears can really add up:

- the fear of missing out
- the fear of disappointing others
- the fear of underperforming
- the fear of making a mistake
- the fear of losing
- the fear of getting injured

The first of these, the fear of missing out (FOMO) is worrying that other people are enjoying their lives and having more fun in that moment than you are (Scott, 2021). You might think that this fear isn't all that bad, but it can actually be pretty damaging, seeing as it can mess with your self-confidence a fair bit. It can also keep you from focusing on things like your practice and training sessions or even games and matches. What if your friends are out having fun at a party while you're running drills? What if you're missing out on some-thing great, while you're stuck at this match?

This kind of fear can easily mess with your priorities and keep you from doing the things you need to be doing to improve your game and strengthen your skills. It can also keep you from focusing on a match or a race, which can ultimately cost you your victory. Suffering a loss is bound to make your FOMO worse because it will be accompanied by thoughts like, "If I'd known I'd lose this game, I would have gone to that party and had fun with my friends instead." Alternatively, FOMO can cause you to actually skip important practices and training sessions, which can again lead to you losing a game. In that case, you'll start having thoughts like, "Would I have lost this game if I had practiced instead of going to the party the other day?" By that point, it will be too late.

Another fear that can mess with your performance is the fear of disappointing others. This is something that a lot of athletes have to contend with. What if you disappoint your teammates? What if you disappoint your coach? Your parents? Your supporters?

Knowing that you've disappointed someone is an unpleasant feeling. It can be quite upsetting, in fact. As such, the fear of it can be really difficult to cope with. It can cause you to start hyperventilating a bit and can start interfering with both your focus and your ability to perform at your best. This can feed into another type of fear, which is the fear of underperforming.

Fear of underperforming can actually lead you to underperform in a game. When this happens, you're likely to experience a lot of self-criticism in the form of thoughts like, "I know I could have made that shot. I'm so stupid, I can't believe I missed!" This is the kind of thinking that is neither encouraging—it's the opposite of that, in fact—nor helpful in the long run.

Moving on, next up is the fear of making a mistake. Ironically, the fear of making a mistake can actually cause you to make mistakes in a game or match. This is a bit like being told not to think of a pink elephant. Let's face it, once you're told this, you won't be able to help thinking of a pink elephant. The main reason why the fear of making a mistake leads to mistakes is that it primes your mind for it. See, the thing about your subconscious is that it actually cannot tell the difference between what's real and what's imaginary. No one's can.

So, when you imagine yourself winning a game, your subconscious believes you're actually doing it and readies your mind and body to achieve it. When your mind becomes preoccupied with thoughts of making a mistake, though, your subconscious believes you're making a mistake or that you've already made one. This primes your mind and body to make a mistake, and before you know it, you've passed the ball to the wrong person.

Sucks, doesn't it? Like the fear of making a mistake, the fear of losing works much in the same way. By thinking a lot about losing, you prepare your mind and body to lose. All of a sudden, your performance level has dropped and you're not able to pull off moves you used to be able to. Your fear comes true, meaning you lose.

Finally, there's the fear of getting injured, which is something that athletes who have been injured in the past are especially prone to experiencing. Athletes who have a fear of injury are more likely to subconsciously protect themselves and keep themselves back from running as fast as they can, or hitting an incoming ball as hard as they can, and the like. Fear of getting injured, then, can prevent you from accessing and using your full potential, and more likely than not, can snatch a golden chance for victory right out of your hands.

Avoiding the Pitfalls

The reason all these different kinds of fears can block you from using your full potential and performing at your best is that they cause you to adopt certain behaviors on a subconscious level. These behaviors chip away at your self-confidence, focus, and source of strength. In short, they prevent you from accessing your full capabilities. So, what exactly are these behaviors and why are they so bad for you?

For starters, your various fears can ultimately cause you to focus too much on your anxiety, rather than your actual performance in the moment (Straw, 2022). This can cause all sorts of problems for you down the line, which is why it's important to learn healthy coping mechanisms for anxiety. Focusing on things like why you feel anxious, how scared you are of losing or making a mistake, and why you can't stop feeling the way you do won't help you to get your feelings under control. Focusing on your game, however, will.

The same logic applies to concerning yourself with how you look to others and what other people—be they your opponents, teammates, or audience—are thinking. This kind of behavior is supremely unhelpful not just because it's distracting, but also because it destroys your ability to play naturally. It interferes with your performance as deep down as muscle memory, which can cause you to make careless, otherwise avoidable mistakes.

One thing your fears often lead you to do is start talking down to yourself. The negative, berating, accusatory, and embarrassed thoughts that run through your mind as a result not only chip away at your confidence but boost your anxiety as well. The more anxious you become, the more negative thoughts you start having and before you know it, you're stuck in a vicious cycle, and you don't know how to get out.

In addition, your fears can ultimately cause you to focus too much on *not losing*. Don't get me wrong: Obviously, you don't want to lose, and there's nothing wrong with hoping to win. But focusing too much on not losing can, yet again, prove to be a massive distraction and distractions are something you want to avoid at all costs. As a general rule of thumb, you should remember that focusing on anything other than the moment you're in, or the game you're playing, is bound to detract from your performance. The more you're able to concentrate on *this* particular moment, the better you'll be able to do.

It can be said, then, that one of the worst mistakes an athlete can make is taking their focus away from the game and becoming distracted by other thoughts and concerns. There are other mistakes that are just as bad, of course, some more specific to rookies than they are to pros and vice versa.

One all-too-common mistake rookies make, for instance, is to hydrate too much (Born, n.d.). This is especially true in the case of endurance athletes, and it can lead to muscle cramping, bloating, and stomach discomfort. As you may imagine, these things can divert your focus from the game you're playing, and therefore, affect your performance. Hence, the importance of avoiding this mistake.

Just as it's important for you to avoid overhydration (and under-hydration, for that matter), it's equally important that you neither consume too many nor too few calories. Doing either can interfere with your energy levels and your ability to do your best on the field. The same holds true when forgoing protein before or after games and even practice sessions. Whenever you're playing a game or partaking in a match, you're relying very heavily on the various muscles that knit your body together. These muscles need protein to function at full capacity. When denied this, not only will they shrink, but they will also whittle down your strength and endurance, causing you to underperform.

That being said, it's important that you don't consume too much food when you're taking a break in a game, race, or match. Otherwise, you'll risk having to suffer through lethargy, nausea, and cramps, which will have defeated the purpose of your eating during your break: to give you more energy and up your game.

Naturally, these are all mistakes that are more typical of rookies than they are of seasoned athletes. That doesn't mean that pros and seasoned athletes aren't prone to making mistakes of their own. They certainly are. For instance, sometimes seasoned athletes get caught up in their training and end up overtiring themselves

(Reaburn, 2018). This is problematic because rest is just as important for an athlete as training. If you overtrain, you deny your mind and body of the recovery time they need. Far from improving your performance, this damages it and keeps you from playing at your best.

Taking a rest, though, doesn't just mean sitting down for a few minutes. It means taking care of your body, from the muscles to the mind, so that it can properly recover. Again, seasoned athletes sometimes forget this glaringly obvious fact. When you don't take long enough breaks, for example, you prevent your muscles from healing and improving as much as they otherwise would. When you don't engage in relaxing activities, like a massage, a hot bath, or meditation, you don't give your body and mind the time they need to decompress. This interferes with your focus mid-game, in the form of pains and aches returning. It also decreases your strength and speed, as well as your endurance levels, which you should avoid doing if you truly aim to become a champion.

3

THE WINNER'S RULE BOOK

The will to win, the desire to succeed, the urge to reach your full potential... These are the keys that'll unlock the door to personal experience.

— CONFUCIUS

Now that you know exactly what mental toughness is, you'll be able to make use of it easily and take your game to levels previously unheard of, right? Well, not quite. Understanding mental toughness is essential to being able to improve it, strengthen it, and use it, of course. But like any skill set, applying it to your life and game is something you need to learn how to do.

The question is, then, how do you use the championship mentality? How can you become a mentally tough person and a tenacious athlete on the way to becoming a champion? Well, to learn a new skill set, you first have to discover what its rules are, just as you have to learn the rules of a game to be able to play it. So, what are the rules to being a mentally tough person and how can you become one?

TOUGH AS LEATHER

You know why it's important for you to be mentally tough if you want to excel as an athlete. But what are the marks of mental toughness? What are those few, choice characteristics that, when spotted in a person, would make you say, "Yeah, they're tough as leather"? There are a few such characteristics, in fact.

Some of these characteristics are what you'd expect. Others might prove rather surprising to some, depending on what their definition of "tough" is. That mental toughness makes people better at managing their own emotions is one such characteristic. Many people think that emotions are a weakness of sorts. As such, they value logic over their emotions and either repress or ignore their feelings.

This is the very opposite of what mentally tough people do. Instead of suppressing their emotions, mentally tough people are able to understand and manage them. They don't, by any means, allow their emotions to take full control of them, of course. A mentally tough athlete, for instance, wouldn't be swept away by their anger after losing a match, not enough to either verbally or physically assault their opponent, for instance. They'd allow themselves to feel their anger, along with any other emotions like disappointment, maybe. Then, they'd be able to process and let them go. In other words, they'd be able to regulate what they're feeling and control their reactions to it (Hutchinson, 2022). Then they'd go over their loss to see what they could do differently in the future, so that they won't experience the same situation and the accompanying feelings again.

A defining characteristic of mentally tough people is that they tend to indulge in productive behavior. What that means is that mentally tough people engage in more active pursuits meant for self-improvement. A mentally tough athlete would be likely to run more drills or additional practice sessions to improve something they're struggling with, for instance.

They'd also be more likely to read for the sake of enjoyment and learning, hit the gym more frequently, listen to self-help podcasts, and even go to therapy (Morin, 2018). This is because a tenacious individual wouldn't consider needing improvement to be a weakness. Instead, they would see working toward their self-improvement as a strength, one that'll up their game, sharpen their skills, and increase both their life satisfaction and their peace of mind.

As you might have gathered from the previous chapter, tenacious people are often able to confront and overcome their fears. This can be as basic as a mountain climber climbing a very difficult route, despite being afraid of heights. It can also take the form of playing a game despite being afraid of losing, or walking out to a match in defiance of the sports or performance anxiety you suddenly feel. Essentially, a mentally tough person will use their fear as a tool that keeps them sharp and alert during their games, rather than seeing it as a hindrance that keeps them back from doing their best.

That being said, there's one thing that mentally tough people aren't usually afraid of and that's making a mistake. This is because mentally tough people recognize mistakes and failures as what they are: opportunities for learning and growth. This might sound a bit odd, but mentally tough people are a bit like babies in this regard. That's a good thing. When babies are born, they aren't able to crawl, let alone walk. In time, though, they figure out how to do the first, then start trying to walk. Mastering the art of walking, however, proves quite hard.

A baby that's learning to walk will fall on their ass quite a few times. Nearly every time, they pull themselves up by holding onto some piece of furniture and take a step or two. Unlike people who aren't mentally tough, they don't let these falls keep them down. They might sob a little if they get hurt, but once they're done, they grab the edge of the couch and pull themselves right back up. They figure out what they did wrong in their previous try, improve their balance, and before you know it, not only are they walking, but they're basically zooming about like an engine has been attached to their back. This is something that mentally tough athletes do as well. They rise back to their feet each time they experience a failure, learn how to improve a move or strategy every time they make a mistake, and so, they keep moving forward.

All this, naturally, has to do with an ability that tenacious athletes have in spades: the ability to self-correct (Hutchinson, 2022). Being able to self-correct means being able to observe your reactions to things—say the opposing team scoring a point, for instance—and then adjusting your reaction to it. This is a vital trait for any good athlete to have, because it prevents them from reacting to events and circumstances in anger or disappointment. It can keep them from becoming provoked, and thus, from losing their focus. Negative emotions, such as anger, can become sources of distraction if you do not learn how to control your reactions to them. If you do learn to control these things, though, you get to improve your performance significantly and attain the victory that you want.

In addition to all that, mentally strong people aren't afraid or even hesitant to genuinely celebrate other people's successes. They can even feed on others' success to manage their own (Strong, 2016). A mentally strong athlete, for instance, wouldn't get upset that their teammate scored the winning shot of a game. Instead, they'd be thrilled. Not only that, but they would know they'd won a part of that victory by passing the ball to their teammate to make the winning shot. Mentally tough individuals, then, don't feel that other people's accomplishments tarnish or diminish their own in any way.

This has a lot to do with the confidence they have in themselves and their own skills. It also has plenty to do with the fact that they focus, not on showing off their skills, but on sharpening them through hard work and effort. Tenacious athletes don't think that they're God's gift to the sports world. Instead, they recognize that they have talent, but that they need to keep pushing themselves to fashion their skills into instruments of surgical precision, rather than blunt objects to blindly swing about.

At the same time, tenacious people have a sense of responsibility, meaning that they're able to accept the consequences of their own actions be they good or bad (Hutchinson, 2022). If they miss a shot or make a mistake during a game, for instance, they own up to it. They don't assign blame to their teammates, or the coach, or the ref. They acknowledge that they made that mistake. This is a very powerful thing to do because it gives you the ability to ask the question "How can I avoid making this same mistake again?" This power allows you to see your areas of improvement and actively work on them. This way, you get to strengthen your weaknesses over time, and you'll be less likely to make that same mistake in the next game or match, and far more likely to achieve the win you want.

This is an extension of yet another ability that mentally tough people have, which is to exhume their past, consciously process it, and learn from it instead of burying or ignoring it. This ability is vital because it makes dealing with past trauma possible. Unresolved trauma is something that can fuel your actions and reactions, without you ever realizing it. It's something that can cause you to take action, or in some cases, refrain from taking action in self-sabotaging ways. This, understandably, can lower your performance and mess with your game along with your ability to rise in your chosen field. When you look to your past and make an effort to acknowledge and work on your trauma, though, you strip it of this power. You reclaim the power and control you have over your own actions, decisions, and goals, and improve both your athletic capabilities and your mental health.

One thing about tenacious people is that they're active problem solvers. This is because they don't get put down or disheartened when they experience a problem. Instead, they hold onto their optimism, shift their perspective, and use their creative thinking skills to resolve it. This is part of the reason why mentally tough people are very resilient. It's also why they're able to overcome obstacles that appear mountainous, and thus, impossible to climb over.

Of course, no one could ever be a good problem solver if they weren't able to actually focus on the problem at hand. Luckily, tenacious people tend to be extra good at focusing. They're able to shut out all distractions (be they internal like anxiety, or external like the booing fans of their opponents) and give their pure, undivided attention to the matter at hand.

This is why, for example, Michael Jordan was able to play the last game he ever played wearing the shoes he wore in his first game with the Bulls, despite the fact that said shoes actually made his feet bleed. He was able to focus on the game through the pain and win, and was massively surprised to find that his socks were soaked in blood afterward in the locker room (Hehir, 2020).

A final, interesting quality that tenacious people all possess is that they aren't afraid of saying "no" to others. This is because tenacious people know how to set firm boundaries and recognize and honor their own needs. They're able to say "no" to a friend when they're asked to a party at midnight, for instance, because they recognize that they need to sleep if they're going to do well in the race they have to participate in the following afternoon. They're able to say "no" to demands made of them that would add stress and anxiety, as well as burdens, onto their shoulders. In doing so, they're able to keep such things from wearing them out. In other words, tenacious people are great at recognizing their priorities and needs and making decisions that look out for them.

Being Tough Isn't Easy

These qualities are great and all, but none of them are easy to adopt or uphold, as you might have guessed. Something as seemingly simple as saying "no" to other people, for example, can be a struggle for many. This is because people are prone to doing certain things and engaging in certain kinds of behavior that run counter to all these different qualities. They're oddly prone to adopting attitudes and thought patterns that damage the strength of their mentalities. These are all behaviors that mentally tough people actively avoid. If you want to become a mentally tough athlete, they're behaviors you have to actively avoid as well. To do so, however, you'll need to know what they are.

One thing that a mentally tough individual would never do is waste their precious time and energy worrying about what other people think of them (7 Things, 2020).

If you don't worry about what other people think, it doesn't mean you don't care what your parents, coach, or teammates have to say. It does, however, mean that you don't allow worries like "What will people say?" to determine your decisions and actions. It means not worrying about other people when you make a mistake or experience a failure. This allows you to focus your energy, which would otherwise have been wasted, on what you can learn from that experience, what you can improve, and how you can grow from it.

Worrying about what other people think can be considered a form of overthinking, which is another thing that mentally tough people don't do. Analyzing the past is all well and good. But overanalyzing it, playing "what if" scenarios over and over in your head, continually beating yourself up for past mistakes, imagining all kinds of potential negative outcomes… All these things are examples of overthinking and absolutely none of them will help you become a better athlete. If anything, such things will disrupt your focus, increase your anxieties, worsen your fears, and on the whole, reduce your ability to perform well. This is precisely why tenacious athletes never engage in overthinking and why you should avoid doing so yourself.

Think of all your favorite athletes, the ones who are considered the best of the best. What do they all have in common? It's not that they've never experienced failure; far from it. Even the greatest athletes of all time have tasted it at one point or another. No, the thing that they have in common isn't this. It's the fact that they never felt sorry for themselves when they did experience a failure or make a mistake.

Here's the thing, feeling sorry for yourself is one of the worst things you can do if you're trying to become a champion. That doesn't mean you're not allowed to feel sad or upset if you lose a match, game, or race. You should allow yourself to feel these things along with whatever other emotions rise up in you. What you shouldn't do is throw a pity party for yourself that will last for days on end, while you keep going "woe is me." Tenacious athletes don't do this. Instead, they let themselves feel their sadness, then process it. The following day, they hit the gym, the track, or the court and get right back to training so that next time, things will turn out differently. They don't deny or repress their feelings, mind you. They just know how to process and cope with them in a healthy way, so those feelings don't keep them from moving forward.

As an extension of that, tenacious athletes refrain from constantly complaining about things. Did they lose a game? They might complain about it a bit afterward, but after that? The conversation will be over and done.

What they will be focusing on thereafter won't be how unfair the ref was or how horrible the other players acted. What they will be focusing on will be themselves. "What can I do differently next time?" they'll ask. "What do I need to work on?" Or even, "How can I improve?" Once they've figured out the answers to those questions, they'll roll up their sleeves and get to work. What if they were to go on tirades for hours, days on end, complaining incessantly about all that went wrong? Well, then they'd be detracting from their ability to honestly ask and answer these questions, work toward sharpening their skills, and learn from their mistakes. Knowing all that you now know about tenacious athletes, would you like to venture a guess as to how many of them would be willing to do that?

Athletes need to rely heavily on their intellect when they're in the middle of a game, race, or match. This is because they have to focus on using the right strategy at the right time and developing countermeasures and strikes against their opponent's moves and strategies. Doing this, though, requires having enough information to work with. It also requires working under the assumption that they can, in fact, be wrong in their judgments.

No tenacious athlete worth their salt would ever jump to a conclusion if they didn't have enough information to work with. Nor would they ever assume that they couldn't possibly be wrong in their conclusion or analysis. They would know that doing the former would leave a blind spot for their opponents to take advantage of. They would also know that doing the latter would result in them becoming too rigid and inflexible in their thinking. This would rob them of their adaptability in a game, race, or match. It would prevent them from switching tactics when they really turned out to be wrong in their judgment, or whenever something otherwise unexpected happened.

Having spoken of flexibility, it's important to note that tenacious people aren't afraid of change. Instead, they embrace it, because they recognize that change—be it in the form of a new teammate, or a new tactic, or a strategy they've never tried before—is a necessary part of evolution. It's essential for any athlete that wants to improve and become a champion. In the sports world, as in technology, for example, change is simply the way of things. Those who understand that and don't resist change get to grow and advance. Those who don't, those who get too stuck in the old way of doing things and resist change? More often than not, they get left behind. It's as simple as that.

John Wooden's Pyramid of Success

Now that you know all that you should and shouldn't do to increase your tenacity, you might be wondering how exactly you're supposed to use all this information to achieve success. This is where John Wooden's Pyramid of Success comes into play. For the as yet uninitiated, John Wooden is a legendary basketball coach. I say legendary both because he made it into the basketball hall of fame and because he invented the philosophical model known as the Pyramid of Success (Derisz, 2022).

The Pyramid of Success is an illustration of the mindset you'll need to achieve success and victory. It essentially breaks down the behaviors, values, and approaches into the 15 building blocks you will need to adopt. It then combines them in a neat framework that you can use.

The Pyramid of Success has five levels in total, all of which are made up of certain building blocks. Below, you'll see an outline of these levels from bottom to top:

1. The base, the very foundation that success is built on, hence it being the bottom layer of the pyramid.
2. Level 2, the cornerstone of gaining the momentum you need on your way to success.
3. Level 3, where building blocks connect the basics to the higher-level skills you'll need to improve your performance.
4. Level 4, which consists of two building blocks that ultimately polish your skills and abilities.
5. The peak, which is where you, as a champion, want to reach.

Now, let's take a closer look at the building blocks that make up these different layers, starting with the base. The base is home to five building blocks, which are loyalty, cooperation, friendship, enthusiasm, and industriousness, respectively. Loyalty means putting your trust in the people around you, such as your teammates and your coach, and being loyal to them. Loyalty is an important building block, because without it a team cannot function properly. After all, how can you go out into the court to play a match if you can't trust your teammates to have your back, and they can't trust you to do the same?

Cooperation is your ability to work with others and share your ideas, tactics, strategies, and more with them. It's essential in solo sports, just as it is in team sports. You cannot get very far in a sport, after all, if you don't cooperate with your coach, trainer, or mentor.

Friendship is, essentially, a support system made up of people that love you. A support system is vital for an athlete on their way to becoming a champion because it can strengthen them when they struggle, which they will do from time to time. And when they're successful, it can share in their joys and victories.

Enthusiasm, meanwhile, is your love and enjoyment of the sport. It's your passion for chasing after your goals and dreams. Without these things, you'll only be able to get so far in your athletic journey before hitting a solid roadblock. Enthusiasm makes industriousness an easier trait to adopt. Industriousness is being a hard worker, and let's face it, you tend to be more willing to work hard if you actually like what you're doing.

How about Level 2, then? Level 2 is made up of four building blocks: initiative, intentness, alertness, and self-control. Initiative is your ability to take matters into your own hands when the situation calls for it. It doesn't mean refusing to cooperate with your team-mates—far from it—but it does mean taking a shot if none of your teammates are able to do so.

Intentness is your ability to keep going when you face obstacles, experience failures, or make mistakes. It's your ability to be resilient in the face of such things and continue on your way with strong resolve. Your alert-ness, on the other hand, is your ability to be in touch with all that's going on around you, even in the chaos of a game. This is something that allows you to make better split-second decisions and judgment calls. You can't very well pass the ball to a teammate, for instance, if you aren't aware that they're open and in a good posi-tion to make a shot, now, can you?

Lastly, your self-control is your ability to avoid tempta-tions that could decrease the quality of your perfor-mance or distract you from your goal. Remember what we said about saying "no" to others? Well, that's part of self-control. It's a skill that comes hand-in-hand with discipline, and you need to be a disciplined individual to excel in your chosen sport.

Level 3 is made up of three building blocks: skill, condition, and team spirit. Your skills are the things you're good at. They're also things you can improve on. They're the set of abilities you can master and sharpen through hard work and effort. Of course, you need to be in good shape mentally, physically, and even morally to be able to do this. That's where condition comes in. Your condition is how well you're doing in these three areas and whether they are aligned with one another or not. You need them to be, if you want to keep improving your skills and moving forward.

Your team spirit's the next level of cooperation, in a sense. This is your willingness to put the needs and success of the team before your own. In team sports, a selfish player will only go so far because their priority will be their own performance, not the team's. A player who has team spirit, on the other hand, will recognize when the team needs to be prioritized to achieve a win. A player who doesn't resent being put on the bench because the team needs another player to step in at that moment to execute a particular move or strategy? That's a player with team spirit, right there.

Level 4 has only two building blocks: confidence and poise. Your confidence is the faith you have in yourself and your skills, as well as your ability to develop and use those skills. Your poise is your ability to stay true to yourself, meaning your values, morals, and the commitments you've made. A player who doesn't let failure get to them and keeps fighting in the face of huge obstacles is one who has poise. So is one who refuses to cheat for the sake of winning, for instance. In essence, then, poise can be summed up as your level of self-respect and composure.

Last, but not least, there's the peak. There's only one building block to be found in the peak and that's competitive greatness. Your competitive greatness isn't just your desire to win. It's your willingness to keep challenging yourself to be better and to become the greatest version of yourself you can be. It's your refusal to buy into the lies told by perfectionism and feelings of inadequacy. It's the focus you have on continual self-improvement while believing in your greatness and understanding that these things aren't contradictory, but are, in fact, supportive of one another.

One of the keys to being your best lies in knowing how to use the Pyramid of Success. You can do this by reflecting on all these building blocks regularly and honestly questioning yourself to see whether you actually possess these qualities or not. If you don't, what do you need to do to possess these traits? If you do, but you don't think they're your strong suits, what can you do to improve upon them? For instance, say that you noticed you weren't great at cooperation, which is a basic building block that you need for success. How can you learn to be more collaborative? What can you do to show your teammates you trust them more? What can you do to show your teammates that they can trust you?

Producing Mentally Tough Athletes

Reflecting on the building blocks of the Pyramid of Success and consciously working on the qualities that you feel you need to improve is one way of increasing your level of mental toughness. But you might be wondering, are there any other methods? Oh, there are plenty:

- setting goals for yourself
- working on building your resilience
- becoming more self-aware
- using visualization
- developing a positive attitude
- training for adversity

While all these different techniques will be covered in significant detail in the chapters to come, let's take a quick look at them now, starting with setting goals for yourself.

Goal setting is important both in the long and short term because it gives you something concrete to work toward. This improves your sense of direction and helps you figure out what exactly you need to do to achieve your goals (Leopold, n.d.). At the same time, watching yourself achieve your goals and being able to track your progress in this way significantly increases motivation. It makes you want to work even harder to see what else you can do, and thus, drives you toward your ultimate goal of becoming a champion.

What about your resilience? Your resilience is your ability to keep working for what you want, even in the face of hardships, obstacles, failures, and roadblocks. It's what allows you to remain optimistic, and thus, figure out a way to overcome the challenges that lie before you. It's what enables you to bounce back from a failure or mistake and come back stronger than ever, which is, decidedly, the mark of a champion in the long run.

As for self-awareness... This is your ability to be conscious of both your strengths and your faults. It's your ability to recognize your skills and improve them. It's also your ability to objectively identify your weaknesses and fix them, strengthen them, or put strategies in place that play to your strengths rather than your weaknesses. It's learning to recognize negative thoughts when you start having them, and put an end to them, thereby preventing them from affecting your mindset, and ultimately, your performance.

Then there's visualization, which is a technique that practically all pro athletes, including the legendary ones, use. Visualizing success is a very effective way of actually achieving it. While the reason for this will be explained in coming chapters, the rule to follow is this: The more realistic and detailed the success you envision, the more effective it'll be, and the better the outcome will be. Visualization is a tactic that goes hand-in-hand with maintaining a positive attitude. A positive attitude is very important because it gives athletes greater confidence and keeps them motivated, whereas a negative attitude would chip away at both of these values.

No matter how great an athlete is, they will face adversity and sometimes struggle greatly against it. This is in the very nature of competitive sports. That's why athletes must train to face adversity. Otherwise, they can be caught unprepared by a particularly strong opponent and flounder as a result. Their unpreparedness is bound to affect them negatively, as it will lower their confidence and make them doubt their own skills.

Training for adversity can be a bit like putting on protective armor. By doing this, you can prepare yourself for any harsh blows that might be dealt to you in the future. Thus, far from being damaged by them, you can work confidently on countering them until you have defeated your opponent and achieved the victory you want.

IT'S TIME TO CHANGE THE MINDSET FROM A FIXED ONE TO ONE OF GRIT AND TENACITY

"Let me tell you the secret that has led me to my goal. My strength lies in my tenacity."

— LOUIS PASTEUR

Now that you have reached this point, you are well aware that achieving absolutely anything you want isn't just down to having a goal, some talent, and a bit of luck. You can even start to see the results of your hard work. But then something happens to send you back to square one... or worse.

What is it that prevents us from the feeling of being unstoppable? From being the best in your field but never taking your foot off the brakes? You know! It's your mental toughness. And you are one step closer to punching past the obstacles and challenges, beating the stress, and growing both physically and mentally. You will still have fears to face but at least you won't hide from them now.

The goal is never to be perfect – but in the world of athletics, you have yourself measure yourself against the rest. Who is that athlete that keeps you on your toes and who are you chasing to beat?

Now imagine what would happen if there was no inspiration and nobody to challenge yourself against.

The truth is, mental toughness is a skill that needs time to develop and not everyone is in the same position as you are. If nobody else can learn this essential skill, where is your competition?

By leaving a quick review on Amazon, you will be able to help other young athletes develop their tenacity and improve the standards of athletics for all!

The more young athletes who can find their mental toughness and keep working on it, the more great athletes there will be. The better they become, the more you can push yourself and exceed your expectations!

PART II

A PRESCRIPTION FOR ACHIEVING MENTAL TOUGHNESS

4

VISUALIZE. WORK. WIN

> *Visualization is the human being's vehicle to the future—good, bad or indifferent. It's strictly in our control.*

— EARL NIGHTINGALE

S o far, we have spent the majority of our time trying to understand what mental toughness is and what it isn't. We have come to grasp why mental toughness is so important for athletes, what benefits and advantages it offers them, and what behavior and traits run counter to it. We've even developed an understanding of how mental toughness works and very briefly looked at techniques we can use to develop it. Now, the time has come to examine these methods and techniques with greater scrutiny, so that we can see how they increase mental toughness and how you're supposed to use them in the first place, starting with visualization. After all, a tool won't be of much use to you if you have no idea what to do with it, will it?

A VISUAL ON VISUALIZATION

Visualization is one of the most effective mindset tools at an athlete's disposal. Don't believe me? Just ask Lindsey Vonn or Michael Phelps. Visualization is the act of using guiding imagery to envision how you want a particular game, match, or race to unfold (Cohn, 2014). That could, obviously, mean visualizing a victory. It can also mean visualizing yourself perfectly executing a move you've been working on for ages. It can mean picturing how a strategy or play that you and your team have developed would play out on the court. In essence, visualization is mentally rehearsing or practicing your performance, skills, or routine to train your body to achieve the victory you want.

The great thing about visualization is that it can be done anywhere, at any time. Lyndon Rush, the Canadian bobsledder, for instance, uses it when he's doing routine, everyday tasks like brushing his teeth or showering. It can also be used immediately before a game, race, or match, which is how plenty of athletes do it. There are many reasons why visualization works.

For one, it actually conditions your brain to attain successful outcomes in a game, race, or match by familiarizing it with the things you want to do. For another, it allows you to play through various different scenarios in your mind. By doing this, you get to dream up different ways that a game could go, including the variety of obstacles and struggles you may face while in play. Now, if you halt your visualization technique in the process of imagining such an obstacle, then it will obviously fail.

But if you play the scenario through in your mind, you'll be able to come up with solutions for how you can overcome those obstacles. You can see exactly how you'd counter unexpected developments, and thus, get a game plan in place. In the process, you'll reduce the number of unknowns you'll face in your upcoming match. You'll eliminate a great deal of anxiety too, since the fear of the unknown is typically a major stressor for most.

"That's great, and all," I can almost hear you saying, "but does that really work?" It does, according to the scientists who researched the effectiveness of this technique. Back in the 1960s, a scientist called Alan Richardson decided to study how effective visualization was in basketball free throws. I'm assuming he chose basketball because he was a fan, but he could have chosen just about any other sport to get the same results.

For his study, Richardson divided his subjects into three groups. He had the first group physically practice doing free throws for 30 days. The second group, meanwhile, only visualized doing free throws for 30 days, and the third group neither practiced physically nor mentally through visualization. The result? Obviously, the third group did quite poorly in free throws, but the first and second groups? The first group showed a 24% improvement in free throws, whereas the second group showed a 23% improvement. That's right, the group that only visualized doing free throws improved nearly as much as the group that physically practiced performing them (Milani, 2019).

How on earth is that possible, though? How can just imagining yourself doing something possibly help you to get better at it? Well, the reason visualization works has a lot to do with how your brain works. Remember what we said about the subconscious and its inability to distinguish between what's real and what's imaginary?

You see, because of this little quirk of the subconscious, performing an action and imagining performing that action both activate the motor cortex of your brain, which is responsible for sending signals to your body to stimulate certain movements (Razmus, 2020). The neurons that are in the corresponding part of your brain fire up. The more those neurons fire up, the stronger the connections they build between them. The stronger those connections, the better you get at performing the movement associated with them, like, say, a free throw.

Visualization for Athletes

Considering the research at hand, it's easy to see that visualization clearly works. But just how important can it be for athletes? I mean, just physically training should be enough to prepare athletes to win victories, right? Survey says, wrong. If you want to be a successful champion and a mentally tough athlete, then visualization is a must. This is because visualization allows athletes to practice and repeat certain moves, strategies, and tactics without overly exhausting their bodies (Quinn, 2018). I mean, think about it. You can only physically practice free throws so many times, but mentally practicing them? That's another story entirely.

But that's not the only reason why you should be using visualization. Remember how we said that goal setting is very important for an athlete? Well, there are two kinds of goals you can set for yourself, as you'll see later on: process goals and outcome goals. Process goals are goals you set for the process of achieving an end result. Outcome goals, on the other hand, focus solely on the outcome of those processes.

As an example, an outcome goal might be "winning the next game with a free throw." A process goal on the other hand might be "throwing the perfect free throw." As you might imagine, coaches, trainers, and sports psychologists all agree that athletes should focus on visualizing their process goals, rather than their outcome goals. This is because the aspect of a game, race, or match that an athlete will have the most control over is the process, not the outcome. There are many things you won't be able to control in a match, from the things that your opponents do to the actions of your teammates. You will, however, always have control over your own actions. By visualizing the process goal, you'll be able to improve your skills, which will eventually lead to the outcome that you want: winning a victory.

There's one other reason why athletes such as yourself should practice visualization: Because it increases your mental toughness. As you may recall, visualization effectively reduces things like anxiety and stress. Anxiety and stress are both things that reduce your mental strength and confidence, all while negatively impacting your mental health (Quinn, 2020). Practicing visualization, then, can help you to avoid all three of these things. At the same time, it can increase your focus during a game, which will, obviously, make performing at your best more achievable.

Here's the thing about confidence... Human beings often need some sort of proof to believe in various things. This includes believing in themselves. Proof is usually something tangible, like a trophy you win, or a point you score. However, it doesn't have to be. Just visualizing a victory, a perfect game, or a great shot can increase your belief in your ability to do all of those things. It can do so because your subconscious will take the images you offer it as reality and believe in them (Niles, 2011). In other words, it will take the saying "seeing is believing" really, very literally. So, the more your subconscious buys into these images, the more you'll start believing in your ability to make them into an actual reality. The more you start believing in this, the more confident you'll become—and the more confident you become? Well, the stronger your mentality will be.

Making It Work

As far as mindset techniques go, visualization is as simple as it is effective. What you basically have to do is close your eyes—you can keep your eyes open in the future but closing them helps if you've never done visualization before—and imagine what the outcome you want looks like. You have to picture how the events that lead to that outcome unfold in your mind, in as vivid and detailed a manner as you can manage.

If what you're picturing starts taking a negative turn, you have to hit pause, the same way you would when watching an actual movie. Then, you have to rewind back to the point where things started turning sour and hit replay there, only this time, focus on painting the picture of a more positive outcome. If you are visualizing a football game, for instance, and see yourself fumbling the ball, you'll rewind to the moment just before that, and picture yourself catching the ball successfully. Make sense?

The more realistic you can make the things that you're imagining, the better visualization will actually work for you. How can you make your visualizations realistic? By using more than your visual senses. To get the best possible results out of visualization, you have to use all your senses. If you're a swimmer, for instance, and are visualizing winning your next race, you wouldn't just see your victory in your mind's eye.

You would also pepper your visualization with sensory details. How does the water feel against your skin when you jump in? Obviously, it's wet, but how cold or warm is it? What about the bonnet on your head and the goggles in front of your eyes? Can you feel that bonnet's tightness? Can you feel the pressure that the goggles are exerting? How about sound? Can you hear the splash of the water as you kick your feet and swim using freestyle strokes? How about your breath? Can you feel yourself sucking it into your lungs each time you turn your head to the side, feel how you hold it in when your face is looking down on the floor of the pool, hear yourself exhale and gulp when you twist your head to the side again? Can you feel your muscles as they strain with movement, your speed as you swim, your fingers touching the edge of the pool when you arrive at the end of your lane?

See how detailed visualization can get with all of those sensory elements? That's exactly what you want to do. You also want to make the images you use as specific as humanly possible. Don't just imagine winning, try to picture exactly how you'd perform a stroke, down to the minutest movement of your fingers as they plunge back into the water. That way, you can improve the movement as much as possible and increase your control and understanding of it.

Now, granted, being able to do all of this at once will take some practice and time. So, don't get frustrated if you can't do it perfectly right off the bat. Instead, keep practicing, rewinding when you need to, and replaying the images you use over and over again. Practice makes perfect, and all that.

In fact, to get visualization to work best, you should try to do it as often as you can. After a while, you'll be able to easily do it when you're washing the dishes, say, out on a walk, or folding the laundry. You obviously shouldn't try visualization when you're doing something that requires your immediate focus, like driving, for example, but other than that? Visualization is a technique that can work any time and should be practiced with regularity. A great time to visualize the way you want things to go is immediately before a game, match, or race. That way, you can go into it with a greater level of confidence and a great deal less anxiety. You can also strengthen your mindset immediately before the game begins, ensuring that you perform at peak condition.

As effective as visualization is, though, you should never use it as a substitute for physical practice. You need to rely on both to excel in your chosen sport and become a champion. While it's true that there's some research indicating visualization can strengthen your muscles to some degree, it cannot strengthen and develop them the same way actual practice can (Quinn, 2020).

Get Inspired!

Having talked about how effective visualization can be, let's give the microphone to the pros to see how, exactly, they make use of it. Take swimmer and Olympic gold medalist Michael Phelps, for instance. Phelps has an entire mental imagery training regimen! This regimen involves watching a "mental video recording" of his races, every single night, right before he goes to sleep. It also involves him doing the exact same thing right after he wakes up every morning. In these reels, Phelps tries to imagine every small detail and every step making up a race, starting with jumping into the water and ending with the victory celebration.

When his trainer feels Phelps needs a little extra motivation during practice, he actually tells him to "play the videotape," which Phelps does. If you're still wondering whether this technique actually works, then all you have to do is take a look at Phelps's record. The fact that he is the most decorated Olympian in history, with 18 gold medals and 22 medals overall should speak for itself (Cohn, n.d.).

Visualization Exercises for Young Athletes

Visualization is a great technique for achieving victory, but that's not the only thing it can be used for. In fact, visualization can help you achieve many different things, like handling pressure better. It can also become an effective relaxation technique, a vehicle for mastering new skills, and a tool for recovering from injuries more quickly. So, without further ado, here are a couple of visualization exercises that can help you to achieve all these things.

Handling the Pressure

Athletes have to deal with a tremendous amount of pressure in their professional lives. This is just as true for pro athletes as it is for young rookies. Given that, learning how to handle this pressure and developing ways to cope are essential for any athlete who wants to be successful. A great way of learning to deal with pressure is to visualize scenarios where you or your team would find yourselves in a clutch (Straw, 2022b).

Let's say you're in a match and there's a few seconds left on the clock. You have the ball, and you have to make the shot. If you do, your team will win. If you miss, or if you're too slow in making your shot, then you'll lose. Visualizing this moment—or a moment of intense pressure like this—can help you figure out how to perform well under pressure. So, start by asking yourself when you'd feel such pressure in your chosen sport. Then, actively and regularly start visualizing that scenario and how you'd deal with it.

Relaxation

A lot of athletes find it difficult to relax before important races, games, or matches. Some even find it hard to relax afterward, their bodies having been pumped full of adrenaline, and all. If this is something you're struggling with, then visualization can help. For this to work best, start by finding a quiet, comfortable place where you can sit by yourself and concentrate, even if it's just a corner of the locker room.

Get comfortable and take deep breaths to induce relaxation as much as you can. Then, picture a scenario where you're completely relaxed, down to its smallest sensory details. This could be getting a massage; it could be sunbathing on a quiet beach. It could be sitting, tucked under a pile of blankets in your living room, staring at the snowfall outside. Whatever scenario you choose, try to make it as vivid as possible and try to experience the positive emotions that it generates as strongly as possible. Keep breathing slowly throughout.

Mastering New Skills

Once you've started learning a new technique or skill, find a quiet, comfortable place and close your eyes. Try not to lie down, as this might prove a bit too relaxing to be helpful. Take deep breaths for 10–20 seconds, and then, when you're ready, imagine a scene in which you're practicing or executing the skill you're trying to develop.

Start by picturing yourself practicing the skill in training first. Then, move on to doing it in a game. This way, you can grow more confident in your skill. As always, make your image as detailed and vivid as you can, and make sure that the skill you're practicing is a resounding success each and every time.

Recovering From an Injury

This exercise is great for athletes who have been injured and are trying to recover quickly for, well, obvious reasons. So, as with the other exercises, find a quiet, comfortable place to sit down and slowly breathe in and out for 10–20 seconds. Then, visualize how you'd look, move, and feel when fully recovered. Picture yourself performing at peak condition and try to imagine how different moves will feel.

5

SETTING YOUR GOALS

If you don't know where you're going, you'll probably end up somewhere else.

— LAWRENCE J. PETER

A goal can be defined as a result that you desire to attain in the near or distant future, through a plan and a set of actions that correspond to it. In layman's terms, goals can be thought of as the things we desire to achieve for ourselves. Goal setting is a must for anyone who has any type of ambition. This includes athletes.

Yet only a very small percentage of people who set goals for themselves actually manage to meet them. One of the main—though by no means the only—reasons for this is that most people don't set reasonable goals. What constitutes a reasonable goal, then? How can you set reasonable goals as an athlete? And once you have, what strategies can you follow to achieve them?

UNDERSTANDING YOUR GOALS

To understand how to go about setting goals for yourself, you must first develop a thorough comprehension of what goals truly are and how they can deliver your dreams. You must understand, for instance, that not all goals are the same. In fact, in the world of sports, goals fall into three distinct categories (Whyte, 2019):

1. outcome goals
2. process goals
3. performance goals

Outcome goals, as the name suggests, have to do with the results of a specific race, game, competition, or match. Winning your next match would be an example of an outcome goal. Process goals, on the other hand, concern the strategy that you follow to perfect or learn a skill. "I will train for two hours every afternoon" is an example of a process goal. As for performance goals, these have to do with how you carry out a specific skill or ability. Shooting a great backhand serve, for instance, would be a process goal.

An athlete worth their salt has to set all three kinds of goals, in both the short and the long term, if they aspire to become a champion. This is because goal setting is considered to be a mental training technique that can increase your motivation, focus, determination, and commitment to the sport (Mackenzie, 2019). Setting long-term goals is a highly effective way of pursuing your dreams. Setting short-term goals, meanwhile, is a fantastic way of figuring out how you're going to meet that long term goal in various steps.

Sports psychologists first noticed how effective goal setting was as a mental tool for athletes in 1968. By studying the different kinds of goals, they were able to pinpoint exactly what kinds of benefits and advantages each of them has to offer. They found that outcome goals, for starters, served as great long-term goals. They also found, however, that they didn't amount to much when athletes didn't choose effective performance and process goals for themselves.

For a goal—any kind of goal—to be effective, it has to be a SMART goal. I say SMART in capital letters because the term is actually an acronym. It stands for: specific, measurable, accepted, realistic, and time-based. As for what those mean and why they matter…. A goal has to be specific in order for it to be achievable. In other words, it needs to be as detailed and vivid as possible.

"Become a world class champion," for instance, isn't a very specific goal, seeing as the definition of a "world class champion" is vague and open ended. So, how can you possibly go about meeting it? "Win gold in the 2024 floor gymnastics," on the other hand, is a very specific goal, because it's concrete.

What does it mean for a goal to be measurable, then? A measurable goal is one that allows you to keep track of how you improve over time. As an example, if you were able to do 30 pull-ups in a row, doing 50 in a row would be a very measurable goal.

An accepted goal, meanwhile, is one that can be shared with other people and accepted by them. If you set a goal for your team to win three championships in a row, for instance, and your team doesn't think they can do it, then that isn't an accepted goal. If, on the other hand, your teammates and your coach are onboard, if they're willing to sign on, to put in the work to achieve this, then that makes it an accepted goal.

You should ask, "Is it realistic?" Can the goal that you have set be realistically achieved by you and your team? If the answer to that question is "yes," then your goal meets the realism requirement. If it's "no," then you're not going to be able to achieve it no matter how hard you try.

Finally, the goals you set have to be time-bound, meaning they need to be achievable in the time frame you allow yourself. Let's say your goal is to win a specific championship. If the championship is only a week away and you've only just started training for it, then I'm sorry to say that it's neither time-bound nor achievable. If you set this goal for yourself a couple of months in advance, though? That means you have more than enough time to put in the work you need to succeed.

Setting goals for yourself as an athlete is vital, whether they're long-term outcome goals, or short-term performance and process goals. Making sure those goals are SMART, however, is even more important, because at the end of the day, a SMART goal is an achievable one.

An athlete who sets SMART goals will be able to realize most, if not all of them. This will have numerous benefits for you, depending on what kind of goals you've set. If you set certain performance goals for yourself, you'll be able to execute the training regimen (process) you need to be able to achieve them. In doing so, you'll improve your performance and your skills. Your improved performance and skills will lead you to achieve certain targets, like winning championships or becoming a pro athlete.

These aren't the only good things that come with goal setting, though. One good, even great thing is that setting goals helps you sort out your priorities. Once you know what you need to work toward, you can go after it. You can sort through everything you have to do, and choose the priorities that'll lead to your goal.

Another great thing about setting goals is that it increases your self-confidence and motivation. This is to be expected. After all, whose confidence wouldn't grow on seeing their skills improve? Who wouldn't be more motivated after reaching targets they hadn't been able to come close to before? But an interesting side effect of goal setting is that it gives athletes a sense of control alongside these things. This makes sense when you think about it. As an athlete, you cannot control the outcome of a race, game or match. There are simply too many variables outside of your control, no matter how good you might be at your chosen sport. This is especially true for team sports. What you can control are your actions and reactions.

Goal setting is something that gives you greater control over these things. It lets you zero in on what you need to do and what you need to improve with laser-like focus. This, understandably, makes you feel more in control of yourself, which in turn, keeps feeding your confidence and motivation, creating a kind of positive feedback loop. Need I say more?

There are certain lessons you can draw from all this. One very obvious rule, for instance, is that your goals should always be as specific as you can make them. Another important one is that you should consider your time limitations carefully when setting goals, as this is the only way to make sure they're time based. If your goal is to win a specific competition, then the time you have to prepare for it is one limitation. So are things like how many hours in the day or week you have to train. The fact of the matter is, you can't set realistic goals or effectively take action to meet them if your time limitations aren't at the forefront of your mind.

As a general rule, your goals should neither be too easy nor too difficult to achieve. Instead, they should be of moderate difficulty, meaning they should provide you with some challenge (Marcatto, 2018). This is because setting challenges for yourself and then overcoming them proves to be incredibly motivating. It also improves your performance considerably. This is especially true for performance goals where you seek to improve your execution of a move. Goals that are too challenging, on the other hand, tend to be demotivating, as they become (or appear to become) impossible to achieve.

One way you can make sure you've set a moderate goal for yourself is to question your perception of it. If you think it's easily done, then odds are, you've chosen a very easy task to accomplish. If it seems impossible, then it's probably too challenging. If it appears to be only slightly more difficult than your average, then that goal is, in the words of Goldilocks, "just right."

Goal setting can be highly motivating, as we said. It can be made even more so if you keep careful track of the progress it pushes you to make. After all, seeing how much you improve, how much stronger, faster, more capable you become through your hard work is something that's bound to energize you. Given that, the more visible and concrete you can make your progress, the better it'll be for your motivation.

The way to make your progress visible is to pick up a pen and a notebook. Let's say you're a long-distance runner and you're trying to improve your time. To do this, you'll need to train and time yourself. To track your progress properly, you should record your time in your notebook and date it. You should record your time in your next practice directly below it and keep going like that after every practice. When you start doing this, you'll notice you've begun to shave seconds off of your time with each practice. After a while, those seconds will accumulate, and you'll be able to track that. You'll be able to see how they eventually lead to you shaving minutes off of your time, and you can celebrate how much faster you've become.

Having long-term goals, like winning the gold at the next Olympics, is great. But you should have short-term ones as well. These goals should be divided between performance and process goals and outcome goals. Think of your short-term goals as milestones or steps you have to take in order to reach your long-term goal. Think of them also as guiding posts, pointing you toward the direction you want to take, if only you'd follow them. You should know, though, that some guiding posts are more effective than others. More specifically, positive goals are better at motivating and guiding you then negative ones are. This is because positive goals have you focus on what you *should* be doing, as opposed to what you shouldn't.

"Be more punctual," for instance, is a positive goal. "Stop being late," is an example of a negative goal. The former is motivating because it's clearer and gives you a solid sense of what you need to do to achieve it. The latter is less clear and can cause you to fumble with what you should be doing. Put simply, positive goals have the power to put you on the right path, whereas negative ones lack that power and can make finding the right path harder than it should be (Hoff, 2020).

At long last the final rule: for a goal to be effective, you have to be able to create a strategy for it. Let's say that you have a performance goal to perfect your backhand serve. What do you need to do to achieve this goal? You need to train and practice. So, you start by putting a training regimen in place. You figure out what you're struggling with or doing incorrectly in your backhand serve. Then, you move on to fixing it. You ask for feedback and guidance from your trainer or coach. You watch videos of backhand serves or watch other people perform them in their matches and games. You analyze what you observe and figure out how to implement what you've learned. You visualize yourself performing the backhand serve, over and over again. Then you physically practice it, again and again, until you can do it with your eyes closed. In short, you devise the best strategy to meet your goal and then you take the steps necessary to succeed.

Setting Goals Like an Olympian

As with anything, there's a step-by-step process for setting goals. This process begins with writing down your biggest goal first. This could be winning the US

Open, the Super Bowl, Wimbledon or any other major competition of the sort. As you can tell, your biggest goal will usually be an outcome goal. It'll also be something you'll be able to achieve in the long term, meaning you won't be able to manage it in the span of a single day.

Your biggest goal should be something that excites you immensely and that you'd be very proud of achieving. This will make you more motivated to keep working toward it. To settle on your biggest goal, you'll have to ask yourself what would excite you. What would you want your greatest achievement to be? As a rule of thumb, your biggest goal should be your highest dream.

That's step one. Step two is to break down that major goal into numerous smaller ones. These goals are the steps you need to follow to achieve your big dream. The small victories you attain on the way to your major goal will accumulate, turning into a sort of scaffolding you can climb to reach your dream. Each smaller victory you attain will bring you one step closer to your major goal while motivating you to keep working hard.

Once you've settled on your smaller goals and constructed a game plan for achieving your major goal in the process, you'll move on to the next step, which is to find a friend to lean on throughout your journey. Having a support system—meaning friends and loved ones—is very important for an athlete. They deal with a great deal of pressure, stress, anxiety, and more, at the best of times. While being mentally tough can help you to deal with these things, having a good friend you can trust and lean on can help too. What's more, it can make you feel supported and loved, which will only increase your mental toughness. All of this will keep you on task as you work toward your goals. It'll keep you from losing motivation if and when you struggle to meet a goal. It'll also make you more accountable for the actions you take when striving for success.

To motivate yourself further, you need to maintain a positive mindset. That means engaging in positive thinking rather than caving in to overthinking and negative thoughts. By sticking with positive thinking, you'll give your mind the strength it needs to push you forward, especially when the going gets tough.

One thing that can further help is making sure to keep things exciting. If you set goals for yourself that you, ultimately, find boring, then you're not going to be all that motivated to meet them. You're also not going to be very willing to work for them and you'll find that you work slowly and less efficiently to meet such goals. Granted, that doesn't mean that every goal you have to meet on the way to your major goal will be as fun as spending a day in Disney World. It does mean, however, that you can make them more fun. If you have to practice for an upcoming game and your goal is to win it, for example, you can turn practice sessions into competitions. That way, you can make them a little more interesting and give yourself some added motivation to do your best.

While you're setting goals for yourself, you should always make sure that they're efficient and measurable. In other words, your goals should always allow you to track your progress, see how far you've come, and grasp how much you've improved. Ensuring that your goals meet this requirement is your next step.

To that end, one question you can ask yourself is "Is this goal quantifiable?" For example, "Do 50 push-ups in a row" is definitely a quantifiable goal. "Do more push-ups" isn't. While you're at it, ask yourself whether the goals you've set are realistic and specific. If you're a tennis or pickleball player, for instance, and you've only just gotten into the sport, "Win the next US Open" probably isn't a realistic goal to set for yourself, though it is specific. If you have been playing tennis or pickleball for a number of years and know that you have five months to prepare for the US Open, though? Well, then, it just might be a realistic goal for you to set for yourself.

Remember how goals need to be moderately challenging to be effective? Well, that's your next step. That means asking yourself whether or not those goals are temporarily out of your reach. The answer to that question should be "yes," meaning that you have to put in some hard work, time, and dedication to be able to meet that goal. This will provide you with the challenge you need and enough motivation to keep climbing up the scaffolding on your way to the top.

Some athletes make the mistake of waiting for motivation to strike, so to speak, so that they can begin working toward their goals. Unfortunately, this line of thinking doesn't get them very far. The thing about sports is that they aren't just about motivation, they're also about discipline. You have to have enough discipline to practice and work hard toward your goal, every day, even if you don't feel particularly motivated that day.

The funny thing is, when you practice in a disciplined manner like this, motivation actually follows. In a weird way, motivation keeps you disciplined, but discipline also triggers your motivation. This reciprocal relationship between the two is one reason why you should always be consistent in your goals and work steadily toward them every day.

The only things you can control in a race, game, or match are your actions and reactions, as you know. Such events are filled with many things that are blatantly outside of your control. That means you can encounter many unknowns, as well as many unexpected turns of events in a game. This uncertainty could take the form of an accident resulting in an injury. It could be in the form of an opponent who's having a particularly good day. It can also be in the form of an unexpectedly good team or something entirely different.

What all that means is that you should account for the unexpected and even plan for it when you're working toward your goals. That way, you can ensure that you'll never be caught unawares and end up scrambling or fumbling as a result. In working toward your goals, then, you should keep your thinking and strategies flexible, so that you can adapt and respond quickly should you encounter an obstacle that you didn't see coming. You should remember that the road to victory is never a simple or easy one, and plan accordingly.

One other thing you should keep in mind is to review your goals periodically. This way, you can adjust or even change them should your priorities, needs, or wants change. You'll also be able to update them if you find that they're no longer challenging enough for you, or if you conclude that they were not challenging enough in the first place. To that end, you should always ask yourself "What's working?" and "What's not working?" Then, decide whether you should change your goals based on your answers.

The same line of logic applies to the strategies you adopt to meet your goals. Like your goals, your strategies should be periodically reviewed. They should take into account new obstacles and challenges you face, new developments that are made in your field—like if a new training technique is invented that you should take heed of—and your changing goals. They should also take into consideration what parts of your strategy have been working for you and what parts haven't, as well as any newfound strengths and weaknesses. Then, they should be adjusted and adapted based on all this information you have gathered.

Get Inspired!

Now that we know how goal setting works, let's see this art form in practice by looking at how actual Olympians use it. Take snowboarding champion, Amy Purdy, for instance. Purdy didn't become an athlete until she was 30 years old. Interestingly enough, she became an athlete *after* losing her legs. Currently, she is a Paralympics bronze medalist, and she owes this success to a ton of hard work as well as her goal-setting skills. In Purdy's view, goal setting is a massively useful tool that allows people to realize what they're truly capable of. It helps them to see their full potential, and by allowing them to gain clarity on what, exactly, they need to do, fulfill it unerringly (Mejia, 2018).

The Olympic figure skater Ashley Wagner is of the same opinion. Wagner, the first American figure skater to actually win a medal in 10 years, believes that your first step to achieving success is finding goals you can aspire to reach (Mejia, 2018). It's recognizing that only you have the power to achieve your dreams, and therefore, focusing on them fully and completely, blocking out everything else, including the sounds of naysayers in the process.

Goal Setting Exercises for Young Athletes

Having discovered the intricacies of goal setting, it's time to put what you've learned into practice. To start things off, let's take a look at one of the more entertaining goal-setting exercises you can do: creating a vision board (Cullins, 2022). A vision board is a great way to start setting major goals, and it just so happens to use the power of visualization. It can be incredibly motivating, not to mention fun, regardless of whether you're working on a physical board or a digital one on a platform like Pinterest.

Assuming you're making a physical vision board, which I would advise that you do, you can start by cutting images out of magazines that represent the things you want to accomplish. You can also surf the net to find more images and print them out. Images like a gold medal or the Fifa World Cup, for instance, wouldn't be too far off the mark.

Once you're satisfied that you have all the images you want, you can move on to pasting them onto a large piece of cardboard. If you want to take this exercise a step further, you can decorate the board with markers, crayons, and the like. Once you're satisfied with your vision board, you'll only have one thing left to do, that is to hang it somewhere instantly visible to you. Hanging it on the wall in front of your bed, for instance, so that it's the first thing you see every morning when you wake up is a great idea. So is hanging it over your desk, so that you can glance up at it as you're doing homework.

Another great exercise you can try is called "One Year from Now." The idea behind this exercise is very simple: It involves asking yourself what your life will look like exactly one year from now (Mead, 2019). Consider your sports career very carefully as you're answering this question. Where exactly in your journey do you want to be a year from now? What skills do you want to have mastered? What competitions, races, championships, and matches do you want to have won? What do you want your relationships with your team-mates (if you have them) and your coach to look like? What do you want your social life, both inside and outside of your sports activities, to look like? How often do you want to be practicing? What do you want to be able to do? What do you want to have improved upon in the year that passed?

You can ask yourself these sorts of questions when doing the "One Year from Now" exercise. You should try to be as detailed as you can when answering them. While describing your life a year from now, write your answers down. That way, you can make them even more visible and concrete. Having written them down, you'll be able to ask yourself the question, "What do I need to do, specifically, for my life to look like this a year from now?" Once you've asked this question, you'll be able to break this large goal into smaller steps. Then, you'll be able to start working on strategies and plans, and ultimately, shape your life into how you imagined it would look by the end of the year.

A final goal-setting exercise you can try is called the "Average Perfect Day." The Average Perfect Day is a great exercise for setting short, daily goals (Nikitina, 2013). It can make both setting them and devising game plans for meeting them very easy to do. You start by taking out a blank sheet of paper and writing down what the perfect schedule would look like for you. This schedule should outline things like:

- your ideal wake-up time
- what you do immediately after you wake up
- what time you have breakfast
- what you do immediately after having breakfast

And more. Your Average Perfect Day schedule should be as detailed as humanly possible. This means it should include actions as small as, "kiss my little brother goodbye before I leave for school," "brush my teeth after breakfast," and "write in my gratitude journal before bed." It goes without saying that the schedule should be realistic, in that it should neither include slaying dragons nor having dinner with Chris Hemsworth (unless you actually happen to be friends with him, of course).

This is a good goal-setting exercise for two reasons: For one, it makes you more aware of your daily habits, which you can then either change or keep as you want. For another, you'll be able to see exactly what you need to do to have the perfect day, then start actually implementing those things into your daily life. In doing so, you'll start setting small but meaningful goals for yourself and actually meet them. These daily goals will bring you one step close to your larger goals with every passing day.

6

SHIFTING YOUR ENERGIES

Nothing can top the man with the right mental attitude from achieving his goal; nothing on earth can help the man with the wrong mental attitude.

— THOMAS JEFFERSON

There's an old saying that goes, "What your mind believes, your body achieves." As an athlete, you might have heard of it. What it essentially means is that an athlete cannot hope to win if they fight with the mentality of a loser. There's a big difference between fighting to win and fighting not to lose. One is a positive mentality that can carry you toward the dreams you seek to achieve. The other is a negative mentality, one born out of fear, no less, that can shift your mental energies and thus, keep you from winning. The importance of your mindset going into a game, race, or competition cannot be overstated. Given that, let's take an in-depth look at how you can achieve the mentality of a true champion.

MINDSET: AN OVERVIEW

Before we can explore the kind of mindset you need to have, we need to first understand what a mindset really is. Your mindset is the mental attitude you have going into a race, competition, or match. It's made up of the kinds of thoughts—positive or negative—that are going through your mind and the emotions they evoke within you (Quinn, 2021).

Having the right mindset, a positive one, is something that can give you a significant edge over your opponents. On top of that, a positive mindset can help you to develop your self-esteem (Mariama-Arthur, 2016). If you want to accomplish something, such as winning a game, then you need to go into it feeling that you can achieve it. To do this, you'll need to have high levels of self-esteem, which you can cultivate through your internal dialogue. If your internal dialogue consists of phrases like "I can do this, I'm good enough to win," then your faith in your abilities will increase. If your internal dialogue is made up of negative thoughts like, "I'm never going to be able to beat this opponent," then your self-esteem will understandably decrease.

There's a similar kind of connection between your mindset and the perspective you adopt going into a match. What you want to do before a race or competition is get into a winning perspective, where you interpret the world around you through the lens of a winner. This is important because the way you see things affects how you react to them. It also affects how you generally behave and whether you're able to remain optimistic in the face of hardship, like a particularly tough opponent. In such a case, an athlete with a winning perspective would fight on and do their best. An athlete who lacked this perspective, on the other hand, would be likely to give up, even if they didn't realize it on a conscious level.

Your mindset, then, can also affect your determination in a race, competition, or game. In the sports world, an athlete's determination is referred to as their drive. An athlete with a positive mindset can harness their drive, meaning they can increase and fortify it. An athlete with a negative mindset, though, would lose their drive, bit by bit, until it's completely gone. Both of these things would obviously reflect in how they played and impact whether they'd win or lose.

An athlete with a negative mindset will lose their drive more quickly in the face of adversity. An athlete with a positive mindset, meanwhile, will rise to the challenge. This is because positive mindsets make people more resilient, and therefore, more able to face adversity. In the process, they're more likely and able to achieve the goals that they set for themselves.

A positive mindset, then, is clearly crucial for you if you want to become a champion. But what kind of positive mindset should an athlete, like you, adopt? On the whole, there are three types of positive mindsets for athletes to choose from (Taylor, 2014):

1. a clear mindset
2. a calm mindset
3. an aggressive mindset

A clear mindset is a kind of mentality where you're not thinking about anything that is related to your game or race. A lot of professional athletes get into this mindset right before a game. They do this because they trust their talent—which is immense—and their level of experience enough to let their bodies completely take over in a game. A clear mindset is one of the hardest mindsets to get into, but it's perfect for those athletes that are more free-spirited, intuitive, and experienced. As such, it's a good mindset to aim for several years down the line, when you have enough races and competitions under your belt.

What about a calm mindset, then? A calm mindset is a great option for athletes who deal with performance anxiety of any sort. This mindset is all about relaxing before a game or race begins, thus, ridding the mind of worries and the body of unnecessary tension. A great first step for slipping into a calm mindset is to turn to relaxation techniques, like breathing exercises and short bouts of meditation. That done, the second step is to use visualization and imagine yourself remaining calm throughout the race. Combined together, these two techniques can help you to activate a calm mindset.

As for the aggressive mindset, while this may sound like a negative mindset, it really is the opposite. An aggressive mindset is one where you're more assertive, forceful, and proactive in a game, rather than passive. It's one where you drive the ball to the net, despite the defensive opposition thrown in your way, or take a chance on a risky shot. In other words, an aggressive mindset is the kind of mentality where you take greater risks (if they have a high reward) and take the initiative to make things happen. Given the competitive nature of sports, an aggressive mindset is a great mental tool that any athlete can slip into and use. In a sense, it can be thought of as a warrior mentality that allows you to win the battles—meaning the competitions—you enter into.

Positive Thinking and Positive Self-Talk

All three of these mindsets—clear, calm, and aggressive —are positive mindsets for you to choose from.

Whichever kind of mindset you prefer, it's essential that it be a positive one if you mean to be a tenacious and successful athlete. Understandably, a positive attitude revolves around positive thinking, which can be defined as your ability to focus on and see the positive of any situation (Sherwood, 2018). So, it's the glass-half-full perspective, so to speak. It doesn't mean ignoring your problems or negative feelings, of course. It just means acknowledging that the good comes with the bad sometimes (as is the way of life), and choosing to expect things, like a competition, to go well for you.

Positive thinking comes with an array of benefits for those who practice it, not just for athletes. These benefits tend to be both physical and mental in nature. The physical benefits that positive thinking offers its practitioners are:

- higher pain tolerance
- lower blood pressure (seeing as it lowers stress levels)
- lower chances of having a heart attack
- a stronger immune system (which high levels of stress would typically take a toll on)
- a longer life span.

As for the mental benefits, these can be summed up as:

- better problem-solving skills
- greater levels of creativity
- more clarity under pressure
- improved mood
- reduced chance of developing a mental health condition such as depression
- better coping skills and strategies

It's easy to see how all these benefits would prove very useful for an athlete. The physical benefits alone can allow athletes to fight for longer and perform better in competitions and races. But it's really the mental benefits that positive thinking has to offer that athletes appreciate. This is understandable. After all, an athlete who is able to think clearly under pressure and has strong problem-solving skills can be a force to be reckoned with in a game or competition. A creative athlete can come up with solutions to all sorts of obstacles and overcome all manner of difficulties to win the day. An athlete who is able to manage their stress and anxiety levels, as well as their fear, can concentrate on their game fully and perform at their absolute best. Put simply, positive thinking can improve athletes' mental capabilities in a way that gives them incredible advantages on the field.

All this being the case, how can you adopt a positive mindset? One of the best ways you can go about using the power of positive thinking is to use positive self-talk. Self-talk is the way in which you talk to yourself in your mind (York Morris, 2016). It's the internal dialogue that's running through there, and it can be positive just as it can be negative. Negative self-talk composed of negative thoughts about yourself can be very damaging to you. Positive self-talk, however, can be incredibly uplifting for you, seeing as it's made up of positive thoughts concerning you.

The defining characteristics of positive self-talk are that it's self-affirming and supportive. As such, it's something that boosts your confidence and self-esteem, increases your drive, and makes you more resilient in the face of adversity and obstacles, including failures and mistakes.

Practicing positive self-talk is a simple thing to do, on the whole, but that doesn't mean that it's easy, especially if you're not used to it. As such, turning it into a regular habit might take some time and consistent practice. One rule you should keep in mind when trying out positive self-talk is that it works better when you refer to yourself using your own name or in the third person, rather than in the first person. That means that saying "Alex will make this shot," or

"Maddie will win this race" is more effective than "I will make this shot" or "I will win this game." Go figure!

A great way to start practicing positive self-talk is to choose a mantra for yourself (Quinn, 2011). This can be something as simple as "You got this" or "Go!" Once you've chosen your mantra, you should make a point of using it frequently and consciously during your training sessions. This way, you can turn it into a habit and make use of the positive feelings it evokes to keep pushing yourself further.

Once you've gotten used to using a mantra, which you can also whip out before a match or competition is set to begin, you can work on expanding it and turning it into a full dialogue. In the process, you can come up with different self-talk phrases that you can use for different scenarios. If you are a mountain climber, for instance, and you are climbing up a particularly difficult route, you can use phrases like, "I'm a great climber." If you're a cyclist and end up taking a bad turn and falling, you can say something like, "Anything can happen at any time. I may have fallen but all I have to do is get up. I can do this."

When you're actively working on your positive self-talk habits, you should craft different phrases for numerous scenarios. This way, you can always have phrases and affirmations on hand when you need them. You can further supplement them, of course, using visualization. When combined or followed up with visualization, positive self-talk can be particularly powerful.

Adjusting Your Thinking

What if you want to be a positive thinker, but your mind is overcrowded with negative thoughts? What are you supposed to do then? This is a common problem that many people face. If you're one of those people, it's important that you work on changing your negative mindset immediately. This is because negative thinking can severely impact your performance in unforeseen ways. For one, it can increase and strengthen the worries and anxieties you may be having before a game and make them infiltrate your mind while you play (Denys, 2022). This can cause you to become distracted and lower your performance.

That's not all, though. Negative thinking can also make you lose sight of the things that drive you, the reasons that you're playing this sport. It can make you lose sight of your goals. Thus, it can result in you losing your motivation to keep going. Negative thinking can also make you give up sooner than you should. It can make you look at the scoreboard and think, "I'm never going to catch up," when you see that you're just a few points behind. In this case, rather than rallying and pushing on even harder, you'd stop trying and lose your opportunity to make a comeback.

Obviously, none of these things make for a champion, now, do they? That's why you have to work on exchanging the negative thoughts you have with positive ones and embracing positive self-talk. To change negative self-talk into positive self-talk, you first have to become aware that you're doing it. This is where mindfulness, which will be covered in greater detail later on, comes into play. Mindfulness can help you to become more aware of your thoughts and thought patterns.

Once you become aware of negative thoughts, you must first actively and firmly put a stop to them. In other words, you need to hit the brakes on that train of thought. You might find this hard to do at first, you might start and stop the same thought processes multiple times. But the more you practice, the easier the process will become. After putting a stop to negative thoughts, you'll move on to replacing them with their positive counterparts. This can be as simple as turning "I can't keep this up," to "I can keep going." If you're a swimmer, for instance, you may end up having to tweak thoughts like "I can't keep this pace up," to make them into "All I need to do is hold this pace steady and I will finish strong" (Denys, 2022).

A great way of countering certain kinds of negative self-talk, which focuses on the things you can't do, is to use positive self-talk, which focuses on what you can achieve. Another is to focus your thoughts on the successful results that you want to get (Cohn, 2017). One last way might be to ask yourself the question "What's the best thing that can possibly happen?" This can detach your mind from catastrophic worst-case scenarios and refocus it on the new outcome that you want. That can, in turn, increase your drive, motivation, and energy, and push you to keep going.

Strengthening Your Subconscious

Here's the thing: Your subconscious plays just as major a role in impacting your attitude and the way you think as your conscious mind does, if not more so. In fact, your subconscious mind has the power to direct your own certain avenues of thought, be they positive or negative, without you even realizing it. Given that, it's important that you understand how you can reprogram and strengthen your subconscious mind, just as you do with your conscious mind through positive self-talk.

Your subconscious is the part of your brain that makes decisions without you consciously being aware of them (Robbins, 2017). If a ball were to fly toward your face, for instance, you'd raise your hands reflexively and that decision would have been made by your subconscious mind. Your subconscious mind governs things like your beliefs and values, including the things you believe about yourself. If you want to shift your mindset from a negative one to a positive one, you have to reprogram your very subconscious, which you can do through several means:

- focusing on gratitude
- embracing uncertainty
- choosing empowering beliefs

Gratitude is an interesting thing in that it can very quickly lessen things like self-criticism, self-doubt, and fear, thereby denying them the power they used to hold over you. In the process, gratitude rewires your very brain to focus on positive things that you should be grateful for instead of negative things that you're afraid of. At the same time, practicing gratitude increases your curiosity, open mindedness, and trust in others. Something as simple as keeping a gratitude journal can do all this and more. Starting the day by listing the things you're grateful for can, in the process, shift your mentality from a negative to a positive one.

Practicing gratitude makes embracing uncertainty easier to do, which is something that can help you to further shift your mindset in and of itself. The thing is, you can never be certain of the outcome of a game or competition, no matter how terrific an athlete you are. Given that, being an athlete and competing brings a certain degree of uncertainty with it. This is something that you need to not only accept, but also embrace. The more you resist uncertainty, the harder it will be for you to overcome anxieties and fears and adopt a positive mindset.

The last thing you can do to reprogram your mindset is to adopt empowering beliefs, rather than self-limiting ones. This is something you first begin doing on a conscious level, by using self-talk. By repeating empowering beliefs, such as "I can handle whatever is thrown at me," or "If something I try doesn't work, I'll simply try something else," you'll be programming them into your subconscious. If you repeat positive beliefs like this enough times, then they'll become part of the very fabric that weaves your subconscious. Thus, they will become empowering beliefs that fuel you and drive your actions, preventing things like fear from overtaking your mind.

Positivity Exercises for Young Athletes

Mastering positive thinking can be hard and it will obviously take some time. There will be moments when you stumble and have to actively fight against your negative thoughts. Luckily, there are certain exercises you can try that will help you ease into positive thinking and quickly get better at it, starting with positive self-talk practices.

Coming up with positive self-talk phrases and dialogues can initially be hard to do. Turning negative ones into positive ones can be even more challenging. Given that, here are a couple of examples of how negative self-talk can be turned into positive self-talk, as well as a couple of phrases for you to try your hand at (Wilson, 2019):

Negative Self-Talk	Positive Self-Talk
I have never done this before.	This is an opportunity for me to learn a new skill.
I'm never going to get better at this.	All I have to do is keep trying and I'll improve.
There's no way this will ever work.	
I don't know how to do this.	
I don't think I can keep this up.	

Now that you've seen how negative thoughts can be turned into positive ones, why not write down some of the negative thoughts you have and work to turn them into positive thoughts as well?

✎...

✎...

✎...

Another thing you can do to promote a positive mindset is to use affirmations. Affirmations are positive statements that further rewire your brain, and you can repeat them on a daily basis, especially when negative thoughts start surfacing. They can be very effective in promoting positive thinking, when done with enough regularity (*The best athletic*, n.d.). Some great examples of affirmations for athletes might be:

- I'm a great competitor.
- I'm highly skilled.
- I can achieve my true and full potential by practicing.
- I'm becoming faster and stronger every day.

Now that you know what affirmations look like, why not come up with a couple of your own?

-
-
-
-
-
-

You can write these affirmations on post-its, which you can then place somewhere very visible, like your bathroom mirror. This way, you'll be reminded of your affirmations every day and by repeating them you'll be able to reinforce the positive messages they give you and really drive them home.

A final exercise you can try is to write down what your best possible future looks like down the line. To begin, simply take out a sheet of paper and write for at least 15 minutes. Try to be as detailed and descriptive as you can in describing your ideal future (Davis, 2021):

✎…

✎…

✎…

Once you're done, keep this document somewhere easily visible and accessible, as it can generate a lot of positive feelings and increase your motivation to keep working hard to obtain the future you want.

Once you're done with your positive mindset exercises, it will be time to move on to your physical exercises. After all, these mental exercises won't help you to achieve much of anything if you don't put in the hours of physical practice you'll need to become the great athlete that you know you can be.

7

TRAINING LIKE A WINNER

The hardest thing about exercise is to start doing it. Once you're doing exercise regularly, the hardest thing to do is to stop...

— ERIN GRAY

A positive mindset is obviously the product of a healthy mind. However, a healthy mind cannot exist within an unhealthy body. In fact, a healthy mindset needs a healthy body to sustain it, if it's to survive. This is one of the many reasons why it's so important that you, as an athlete in your prime, take care of your physical fitness along with your mental health.

Taking care of your physical health, though, can look a little different for athletes than it does for regular human beings. After all, athletes work out regularly, not to mention more intensely than the average human being, meaning their body requires different kinds of nourishment, greater calories, and more care than you'd think. So, what are the best ways of taking care of your physical health? What do you need to do to get into the best shape of your life, thus increasing your conditioning and performance, without putting undue stress on your body? Let's find out!

EXERCISE TO LIVE

Exercising regularly is one of the best things you can do for yourself, even if you aren't an athlete. This is true for both your physical and mental health. For instance, did you know that regular exercise improves brain function, meaning your abilities to think and remember things (Gavin, 2018)? Did you know that it also improves the quality of your sleep and makes it easier for you to fall asleep at night?

How about the fact that it lowers your risk of developing a mental health disorder such as depression? That might sound odd, but it starts making a little more sense when you think about how exercise causes your brain to release feel-good chemicals such as endorphins. Endorphins make you feel good, lower stress levels, and even act as pain relievers, so it makes sense that a person whose body is flushed with endorphins would be less likely to feel depressed, does it not?

Naturally, exercise also comes with an array of physical health benefits. It's a known fact, for instance, that it helps you to lose weight, prevents you from developing conditions like type 2 diabetes, as well as heart disease and high blood pressure. That it strengthens your muscles is a given, but exercise can even strengthen your bones. To top all of that off, in recent years, scientists discovered that exercise helps you to age well and makes it easier for you to keep moving around and leading an independent life when you get to be older (Gavin, 2018).

Clearly, then, exercise is one of the best things you can do, but how much should you exercise? Is there such a thing as too much or too little of it? If you're between the ages of 6 and 17, for instance, experts recommend that you exercise vigorously for 60 minutes a day, three times a week (*How Much Physical Activity*, 2020). One of the key words there, you see, is "vigorously." So long as those hour-long exercise sessions involve you doing some vigorous activity like running or working out in the gym, then you can do whatever kind of exercise you'd like. You can tell that your activity level is vigorous if your heart is beating fast, your breathing is deep and fast, and you're working up a mild sweat (Mayo Clinic, 2021).

Fit and Fabulous

So, that's the recommended level of exercise for mere mortals. What about budding athletes such as yourself? Well, athletes have to work out more often than other people do to keep in peak condition and become the best possible versions of themselves. This requires following certain training regimens.

Everyone's regimen is slightly different, of course, based on their body's specific needs and what kind of sports they're engaged in. Yet, the broad strokes of professional athletes' training regimens are the same. A typical pro will spend five to six hours a day, six days a week, in training (Suchde, 2013). The training, of course, won't just be overly long, compared to a regular person's workout. It'll also be intense and grueling. The warm-ups that a pro does, alone, would give the average human being chills. This is because every single training session is treated as an actual competition or race, in a sense. Pro athletes train as though they're trying to win a championship at that very moment, so that they can push their endurance and condition levels to the max. In doing so, they get their bodies running on high-intensity levels, which is what they need to win a race or competition.

That doesn't mean, however, that pro athletes don't know how to take a break. If anything, they recognize better than non-athletes how important breaks are. That's why they keep their training regimens varied. Think about it like this: If you were to start hitting the gym regularly, you wouldn't focus on working out your legs exclusively, not unless you wanted to end up with massive thighs and a noodle-thin upper body, anyways. Instead, you'd alternate between muscle groups and try to work on them equally. Pro athletes basically do the same by alternating between strength, endurance, and stamina training during their sessions. They try to keep their training as well-rounded as they can so they're as prepared as they can be for their next victory (*How pro athletes train*, n.d.).

Considering how intense pro athletes' training sessions are, it would be unrealistic to expect a young, relatively new athlete to emulate them, particularly if they're also juggling things like high school and homework alongside their sports careers. That doesn't mean, however, that rookie athletes don't have anything to learn from the pros. To the contrary, they do. The primary lessons that a young athlete can draw from pro athletes can be summed up as follows, at least for the time being (Barroso, 2016):

- **Do jumping exercises**

Jumping exercises, like jumping jacks, are great because they're a huge part of most sports, from boxing to volleyball, basketball to gymnastics. As such, getting accustomed to jumping and managing weight shifts in the process is an invaluable part of your training. Such exercises are also really good for teaching your body how to transfer force to the ground and for increasing your conditioning.

- **Train with others**

If you can, you should always train with others, even if you're not in team sports. Training with others will naturally cause an athlete's competitive streak to kick and thus make them go harder during their practice sessions and workouts. It will also provide them with someone who can spot them and help to either perfect or correct moves, if they're making a mistake without realizing it.

- **Hydration, hydration, hydration**

Obviously, you're going to be getting quite sweaty in your training sessions, unless, of course, you happen to be doing laps in the pool. Even if that's the case, though, you should always make sure you drink plenty of water when you're training. Your muscles need that water to lubricate themselves, which means that the more water you drink (within reason) the more you reduce the chances of an injury, by, say, pulling a muscle.

- **Take breaks but stay active while you rest**

Rest is an important part of any training or workout session. You're not a machine, which means you cannot keep going indefinitely. Actually, even machines can't keep going indefinitely, seeing as they get overheated. What that means is that you should take short breaks throughout your workout sessions.

As a general rule, you can take breaks after a particularly vigorous or strenuous burst of activity. When you're taking these breaks, you should remember that one of the worst things you can do is to sit down or, heaven forbid, lie down. Doing either of these things is a bad idea because they can cause your blood pressure to change suddenly. What you want to do during your rest periods is to lower your heart rate slowly, which is why you should be moving around. If you have a 10-minute break, for instance, you should be spending it slowly walking around, even if your legs feel tired, rather than crashing on the benches.

Fit in Five!

Having said all that, you need to focus on improving five very specific things when you're working out.

These are your endurance level, movements, strength, speed, and recovery.

Your endurance, otherwise known as your stamina, is your ability to keep going under strenuous conditions. You need your endurance levels to be high if you want to be a great athlete, since you need to run, jump, kick, pass, and leap all over the place when you're in a match or race. If you're a basketball player and your endurance levels are low, for example, you're not going to be able to last throughout the entire game, what with all the running you'll have to do to chase after the ball.

You can increase your endurance level by doing cardio workouts. If you're new to cardio, or if you're just at the beginning of your training session, you should kick things off slowly. Then, you should increase the intensity of your training bit by bit. What you want to do is to increase your heart rate gradually, rather than go from 0–100 in two seconds flat. A good strategy to follow is to do moderate intensity cardio for about 15 minutes. You should be breathing a little heavily at this point, but you should still be able to talk. After that, you should slowly make your workouts more intense until you reach your maximum level (*Three ways young athletes*, 2016).

Now, on to your movements. When you're training, you want to repeat movements that you'd be doing in a game or competition and mimic them as closely as possible. Some of these movements, though, don't have corresponding equals that you can execute in the gym. Given that, you should focus on doing compound movements (like squats and deadlifts) that engage multiple joints all at once.

The beauty of compound movements is that they teach your body how to absorb force—like when you catch a basketball that has been passed to you or receive a volleyball—and apply it to the ground. As an added bonus, such moves engage multiple major muscle groups in one go, thereby ensuring you get to strengthen all of them at once. This way, you can train your muscles to execute the movements you'll need to do perfectly when the time comes.

Once you've perfected your movements, you want them to be as powerful as humanly possible. This requires working on your strength. This is why athletes such as basketball, football, and soccer players hit the gym regularly. They want to pack more of a punch with their shots. Before you start doing strength training, which you can do with either weights or using your own body weight, you should consult your coach and your doctor (Gavin, 2018). That way, you can learn what muscle groups to train and how. The muscle groups that a volleyball player needs to train will be very different from those of a skier, swimmer, or soccer player, after all.

After you've consulted your coach and doctor, you can ease into a strength training routine. If you're new to strength training, you should opt for exercises that don't require weights. You should use your own body weight instead. In time, as you perfect the movements involved and get stronger, you can start adding weights to the mix and slowly increase their size. You should try to do 8–12 repetitions of each movement with or without weights. As you're training, you should always have a trainer or a training buddy with you. This way, you can ensure you're doing all of the moves correctly and avoid an injury. You'll also have someone to spot you when you're lifting particularly heavy weights.

Increasing your speed is vital in most sports as well, and there are numerous ways that you can do this. The first thing to pop into your mind when someone says "speed" is probably cardio. But that's not the only way you can start picking up speed. There are many other drills that can help you to achieve the same results. Cone drills, for instance, can be a great way of doing this. The advantage of these drills is that they allow you to break down various moves associated with your sport and combine them with speed practice sessions.

Cone drills that involve dribbling are an obvious example of this (Gleason, 2018).

Finally, there's recovery... That's the time period you give your weary muscles to recover from the exhaustion and wear and tear they experience during training. Giving yourself enough time to recover is highly important, because if you don't, you won't be able to reap the benefits of your training, no matter how hard you push yourself. That means that you have to get enough sleep at night, so that your muscles can knit themselves back together, and so you'll be able to concentrate when competing in a match or race. You also need to watch your diet, making sure to eat nutrient-rich food—especially proteins that your muscles will need—so your body gets all the fixings it needs to become stronger (*5 practical self-care*, 2019).

Dealing With Demons

Working out isn't always the most fun thing to do. Sometimes getting out of bed and hitting the gym is the thing you least want to do in the whole world. While this is understandable, it's important that you push through it and get your workout in regardless. Considering how hard doing so may be, though, it's important to have strategies in place that can get you going (Waehner, 2021):

- Promise yourself a reward after your workout. That can give you the external bit of motivation you need when your internal motivation is lagging.
- Hire a trainer or get a workout buddy. Either can make you more accountable, committed, and give you some external motivation.
- Remind yourself of your outcome goals—e.g., win the world cup—to remember your motivations and let them drive you forward.
- Plan your workouts ahead of time and work them into your schedule. Stick to a routine so you won't have the "I don't have time to work out today" excuse.

What's one of the best ways to get yourself off the couch and to the gym? It's to remind yourself that this is the only way to perfect your skills. When you work out, you give yourself everything you need to develop your abilities and improve your performance and moves. As you improve your moves, your confidence in them naturally grows, and we already know how important confidence can be for an athlete. In fact, the confidence and trust you have in your moves can mean the difference between winning and losing. Take the football player Ben Simmons as an example. Simmons used to be known for his hesitancy when performing jump shots because he missed more often than not. A couple of years later, though, he became known for his jump shots.

Why was Simons suddenly able to make jump shots? Because he put in the training he needed to improve them, and he put his faith in his ability to execute them. That trust removed any hesitancy he felt in the game, which ultimately improved his aim and the force of his shots. This is where the power of training and trust lies for an athlete, which is why you need to keep a regular workout routine and trust in your abilities (Cohn, 2021).

Training Exercises for Young Athletes

By now, the importance of training should be blatantly obvious. Seeing as that's the case, let's take a quick look at some of the exercises you can try to improve your game. If we're talking strength training, for instance, some of the best exercises you can try are (*The 8 Best*, n.d.):

- push-ups
- elevated squats
- trap bar deadlifts
- leg deadlifts
- half-kneeling arm presses

If you want to increase your agility, on the other hand, you might want to give the following exercises a try (*Best agility training*, n.d.):

- cone dribbles
- figure-8 crossovers
- run-shuffle speed drills

If you want to improve your balance and stability, though, the exercises you should consider are (Bracko, n.d.):

- front planks
- seated dumbbell overhead presses
- squats and lunges
- single-leg balance

8

MEDITATION + MINDFULNESS = MENTAL TOUGHNESS

We've heard the term "mindfulness" a few times in this book by now. Mindfulness is your ability to be fully present in a given moment and aware of what's going on, both internally and externally. This means being aware of all that's going on with your teammates and opponents in a game, as well as all your positive and negative thoughts and feelings (Mindful, 2020). Mindfulness is an incredibly useful tool for an athlete to have. This is because it can offer them a wide array of benefits:

- reducing their stress levels, which reduces negative thoughts
- enhancing their performance by allowing them to fully focus on the moment and what they're doing
- allowing them to gain insight, by making them aware of their negative and positive thoughts, as well as their strengths and weaknesses
- making it possible for them to be self-observant
- eliminating self-criticism and negative thought patterns by making it possible to see that mistakes and failures are learning opportunities
- inspiring curiosity by making them more open minded and thus able to learn new things

Athletes who practice mindfulness reap all these benefits and more when they're competing. They also gain a valuable way of managing stress and other negative emotions, developing healthy coping mechanisms, and in the process, reducing the possibility of experiencing mental health issues like depression (Scott, 2022).

MEDITATION

One of the chief ways of developing mindfulness is to practice meditation. Meditation is a proven method of increasing your mindfulness, self-awareness, and focus, while decreasing your anxiety and stress levels (Star, 2018). Meditation is able to do all this because it trains your mind to consciously focus your attention on the present moment (Mayo Clinic, 2020). It does so by making you take note of how you feel, what you think, how the sensation of the ground beneath your feet and the temperature of the room feel, what sounds you can hear, what you can smell in the room, and more. By actively focusing on all these little things that you'd typically be blind to, you train your attention to take in greater detail and become more aware.

To train your mind in this way, you must first get into a comfortable position in a quiet setting so as not to be distracted (Star, 2018). This can mean sitting down on a comfortable mat, or a couch, or even lying on your back. Once you're in position, you need to relax your breathing. This means taking deep, slow, regular breaths from the diaphragm so that your lungs expand to full capacity (Mayo Clinic, 2020).

If you're new to meditation, then odds are that all sorts of thoughts are going to be flitting in and out of your mind. The trick here is to divert your attention from them and focus it on the moment and all the sensations you're feeling. It's to allow your thoughts to pass on by, without chasing after them. This can be difficult to do at first, so bringing your attention back to your breathing might be helpful. If you find it hard to keep concentrating on the moment or your breathing for long periods of time, then you should try to keep your initial meditation sessions short. One to two minutes should do. A week later, you can increase your meditation time gradually, until you can do it for 10, 15, 20 minutes at a time, if not longer.

As for what type of meditation you should try, you have a great many options to choose from (Mayo Clinic, 2020):

- **guided meditation,** where you use visualization and keep your focus on imagery or scenarios you find relaxing
- **mindfulness meditation,** where you pay attention to all the sensations, feelings, and thoughts that you're experiencing without fixating on any of them
- **mantra meditation,** where you keep repeating a chosen mantra (which can be either a word or phrase) while you meditate and keep your focus on it
- **tai chi,** which is a kind of martial arts that uses mantra meditation
- **transcendental meditation,** which has you repeat your chosen mantra in a very specific way throughout the practice
- **qigong,** where you combine meditation with breathing exercises, and focus on specific, flowing movements while maintaining your balance

Whatever kind of meditation you go for, the practice will be incredibly beneficial for you as an athlete, and not just because it will reduce your stress levels. There's also the fact that meditation improves the quality of your sleep and speeds up your recovery time after workouts or injuries, all while increasing your endurance levels (Keim, n.d.). This is why famous athletes such as LeBron James, Kobe Bryant, and Michael Jordan all meditate regularly and why you should as well (Grabowski, 2020).

Meditation Exercises for Young Athletes

Meditation can be a tricky thing to get into, not the least because you're likely to get a little restless when you first sit down to give it a try. If that's the case, and if you've never meditated before, here are a couple of meditation exercises to get you going:

- **Basic Meditation**

Try to sit down at the same time every day—whether it's morning, afternoon or night is up to you—to meditate. Set your time to 12 minutes, get into a comfortable position and start taking deep, slow, relaxing breaks. Try to keep your attention on your breath as you meditate. If you struggle with this, you can play some soothing music or white noise (like the sound of waves in the background) and focus on that. Try to notice when your mind drifts away, and instead of chastising yourself for it, gently bring it back to the moment and keep going until your 12 minutes are up (Reynolds, 2017).

- **Focused Meditation**

This meditation can be a great way of increasing your focus and attention. As always, it starts with getting into a comfortable position and staring at an object of your choice (Focus Meditation, 2022). For argument's sake, let's say it's a vase. When you start meditating, keep your gaze fixed on the vase and try to notice every single detail about it, from how it's designed to what it's made of. Pay attention to how the light in the room is hitting it and where its shadow falls. Try to keep going like that for about 10 minutes, though you can keep your initial meditations a bit shorter than that.

- **Yoga Poses**

Strike a pose! If you find yourself getting a little restless when meditating, you might want to give yoga poses a shot. Yoga poses, like the downward facing dog, the chair pose, and the bridge are great moves to explore. This is because yoga has you actively practice meditation while stretching your muscles and joints, thereby making you more flexible. This helps prevent injuries and teaches you how to harness the power of your breath, all while increasing your awareness, mindfulness, and focus levels (Bekkala, 2015).

9

FORMING A PRE-GAME ROUTINE

Success is the sum of small efforts, repeated day in, day out.

— ROBERT COLLIER

There's one last thing an athlete has to do if they want to increase their mental toughness and become a champion: They have to establish a regular routine for themselves and live by it every day. Routines may seem tedious from time to time, but they're an essential tool for improving both your mindset and your performance. Simply put, having a set routine can help you transform from just any other player to one of the best.

THE POWER OF ROUTINE

Routines are very powerful tools for one very simple reason: They ensure that athletes are totally and completely prepared for the games they'll play and the competitions they'll participate in. Routines improve performance and make sure athletes can fight in the best possible shape (Taylor, 2012).

Athletes have two kinds of routines: training routines and pre-competition ones. A training routine is the schedule, order, and way in which you practice on a day-to-day basis. It usually starts with a warm-up period where you get your body ready for the workout you're about to put it through. Then, you'll move on to low-intensity practices, followed by exercises and drills that keep getting more and more intense. These drills and exercises are, of course, very focused, specific, and goal-oriented—the goal being for you to perfect the moves you're working on or become faster and stronger when executing them.

Pre-competition routines are a little different. These are like regular routines but done closer to a competition or match. Hence, they tend to be far more intense. They also last longer and can sometimes go on for hours.

Routines are important for all athletes, but especially young athletes who are at the very beginning of their careers. This is because routines can be a way of establishing strong habits that can last a lifetime (Cohn, 2014b). Establishing a practice routine means committing to performing the same actions regularly. This helps young athletes automate the moves they have to perform in competitions. It helps to turn them into reflexes, so they can perform without even thinking about it. When a movement, like an uppercut, for instance, becomes automatic, executing it saves you time. It allows you to move faster than your opponent and thus score the point that you need to score. Put bluntly, a routine basically becomes the blueprint you'll follow on your way to winning.

So, what should a winning routine include? To answer this question, we'll have to take a page out of Olympic athletes' books. Most Olympic athletes, such as the diver Kassidy Cook, for instance, would agree that a good routine is one that allows you plenty of rest (Wolfe & Lastoe, 2020). This means that your routine should let you get the daily dosage of sleep your body needs and engage in self-care activities like filling the tub to relax and ease your stress.

A good routine should also make plenty of space for healthy eating habits, at least according to tennis player Novak Djokovic. That means choosing nutritious food and establishing actual meal and snack times to keep your energy levels up. Meanwhile, soccer player Carli Lloyd believes that your routine should include a set time for visualization. Considering how important visualization is for an athlete, this makes an abundance of sense.

Achieving a Winning Routine

A winning routine starts the moment you wake up. A great way to begin your routine is with a couple of deep-breathing exercises or meditation. Once you're up and at 'em, it can take the following steps (Nolan, 2018):

- smiling at yourself and repeating your self-affirmations into the mirror

- drinking a full glass of water before having breakfast
- doing stretching exercises
- having a healthy breakfast

Next, you'll move on to all the "to-dos" making up the rest of your routine. For this, you'll need to have some excellent time-management strategies in place. These strategies will keep you from spending too much or too little time on a single task, to the detriment of all else (*Time management*, 2018):

- working on your daily plan and going over your tasks every morning
- planning your weekly and monthly schedule and accounting for important events such as exams and birthdays
- figuring out the best times to do things like homework—some people, for instance, are more productive when they work after dinner, while others are more productive if they get to work as soon as they've gotten home from school
- scheduling in breaks and free time so you can relax, socialize, and have fun, all of which are important for your mental health, productivity, and stress management

- accounting for things like travel times—how long it takes you to get to practice, for instance —and being realistic about them

Preparing for the Competition Days

Those were some strategies for your regular routines. But how about competition days? Is there anything you can do to prepare yourself for those? There are, in fact, many strategies you can turn to. Some of these are good for mentally preparing yourself before the competition begins. Others are great while the competition is going on. Some even work well after competitions. Here are some ways to prepare yourself before a competition (Wensor, 2017):

- Make sure you have packed everything you'll need to have with you at your competition. No one wants to realize they've forgotten to bring their water bottle five minutes before the competition begins.
- Bring healthy snacks and plenty of water with you.
- Warm up properly before every competition.
- Check the weather forecast before a competition so you can prepare accordingly.

How about the things you can do during a competition? Well, these can be summed up as (Asics, 2016):

- focusing solely on your technique and the moment you're experiencing instead of whether you're winning or losing
- visualizing your performance during breaks
- using your stress-management techniques to prevent stress, anxiety, and fear from overtaking your mind
- using positive self-talk in the gaps that the game allows, particularly the breaks
- making sure you hydrate and snack to keep your energy up

- having fun and enjoying the game

Lastly, these things should absolutely be a part of your after-competition routine:

- cooling down after the intense workout you just had
- walking around a bit to get your heart rate to slowly calm down
- congratulating your opponent for a good game
- allowing yourself to feel whatever emotions you're feeling, even if it's sadness following a loss
- reminding yourself that just because you lost this game doesn't mean you're a bad athlete, it just means you have something to learn and an opportunity for growth
- taking a nice long shower
- getting some much-needed rest
- going back to practice the following day (or the day after that)

Get Inspired!

Sticking to your routine requires having a certain level of discipline, as you may have gathered by now. This is something pro athletes have in spades. If you want to be mentally tough and successful like them, it's something you need to have as well. Don't believe me? Then take Lionel Messi, the star soccer player as an example. Messi is an Argentinian player whose name is known the world over. He has won the Ballon d'Or six times and is one of the most disciplined players in the world (*Most disciplined*, 2021). This is why he has pitched for 800 games. It's also why he only received a single red card in all his career.

Messi received that card toward the very end of a game when he punched another player in the back of the head in frustration. This was a rare moment for Messi when his discipline slipped, hence the red card. For an athlete, discipline is vital because it can keep them from becoming victims of their own frustration, stress, and anxiety, as Messi did in this case. It can also help them to practice very dedicatedly and regularly and so, improve their talents faster than anyone can ever believe.

Exercises for Young Athletes

Athletes need to develop several kinds of routines for themselves. One of these is the warm-up routine. Warm-up routines are important because they get your muscles "warmed up" and make it less likely that you'll suffer a soft-tissue injury (*Warm-up routine*, 2020). They also make your heart rate climb slowly before the game, so you don't have to go from 0–100 instantly. Depending on what kind of athlete you are, a good warm-up routine might look like this:

- walking lunge—5 reps for each leg
- lunge with a twist—5 reps for each leg
- walking lunge in reverse—5 reps for each leg
- jumping jacks—15 reps
- tall lateral shuffle—over 10 to 20 yards
- low lateral shuffle—over 10 to 20 yards
- stretches

Your warm-up routine is a part of your game-day routine, which starts from the moment you wake up. A typical game-day routine might look something like this (Guyer, 2022):

Morning

- wake up
- brush your teeth
- stretch with gentle movements
- take a cold shower
- meditate/do a breathing exercise/write in your gratitude journal
- have breakfast

Before the Game

- get dressed in the locker room
- do your warm-ups
- have a pre-game snack and drink a little water
- do your visualization techniques
- practice positive self-talk
- do your relaxation techniques
- begin the game

After the Game

- do your cool downs
- congratulate your opponent (whether you won or lost) for a good game
- write down four things you did well in this game and one thing your can improve on

- drink lots of water
- take a shower
- eat a good meal
- go home and rest

Now that you know what a good game-day routine looks like, why not write down one of your own for practice?

✎...

✎...

✎...

CONCLUSION

You've been introduced to many different techniques throughout this book that can help you to become a truly great athlete. From visualization to creating a routine that works for you, there's no end to the things you can do to improve upon your strengths. As different as all these methods are, though, they all have one thing in common (as you might have noticed): They all increase your tenacity in one way or another.

Tenacity or mental toughness is vital for any athlete that wants to rise to new heights. It is, after all, what allows athletes to overcome their fears and anxieties, gain faith in their own abilities, and learn from their mistakes and failures. It's what makes them resilient and confident in the face of adversity and setbacks. It's what allows them to manage their stress, so it doesn't cloud their judgment or mar their abilities. It's how they regulate their emotions, so they're not swept away by them mid-game, and they can focus fully on their performance. Put simply, tenacity is the mark of a great athlete in the making as it enables them to give the best performance of their lives any time they step up to compete.

All of this and more is why it's vital that you work on raising your mental toughness and becoming a truly tenacious athlete. Only in doing so can you reach the heights that you dream of. Luckily, now that you have gotten to the end of *Tenacious*, you know exactly how to go about doing that. That means you only have one last question left to answer before you can close this book and get back to practice: Are you ready to begin?

Thank you for reading *Tenacious*. I hope you enjoyed this book and found it to be useful. If you did, **please leave a review!**

GLOSSARY

Adrenaline: A hormone that makes your heart and breathing rates go up and prepares your muscles to do tiring work.

Anxiety: A state of nervousness, worry or unease.

Cortisol: A hormone that makes your blood sugar rise, makes the brain use more of said sugar, and gives your body more of the substances needed to repair wounds or injuries.

Drive: An athlete's determination.

Grit: An athlete's ability to thrive under adversity.

Mental toughness: Your level of resilience and self-confidence in a competition.

Mindset: The kind of attitude you adopt when going into something like a competition.

Overthinking: Thinking about something excessively and for too long.

Performance: Your ability to carry out the physical actions required by the sport activity you're involved in.

Pro: An athlete that is paid to play sports for a living.

Rookie: A newcomer to a sport.

Stress: The physical and physiological response your body gives to a perceived threat.

Tenacity: Mental toughness.

REFERENCES

Asics Stories. (2016, November 15). *Mental preparation & training for athletes*. ASICS Blog. https://www.asics.com/in/en-in/blog/article/6-winning-ways-athletes-mentally-prepare-for-competition

Barroso, M. (2016, August 26). *10 ways to train like a professional athlete*. Men's Journal. https://www.mensjournal.com/health-fitness/10-ways-to-train-like-a-legend/

Bekkala, A. (2015, July 7). *7 yoga poses for young athletes*. ACTIVEkids. https://www.activekids.com/parenting-and-family/articles/7-yoga-poses-for-young-athletes/slide-6

Best agility training workouts for youth athletes. (n.d.-a). VertiMax. https://www.vertimax.com/blog/best-agility-training-workouts-for-youth-athletes

Born, S. (n.d.). *The top 10 biggest mistakes endurance athletes make*. Hammer Nutrition. https://hammernutrition.com/blogs/essential-knowledge/10-biggest-mistakes-endurance-athletes-make?_pos=1&_psq=10+biggest&_ss=e&_v=1.0

Bracko, M. (n.d.). *Getting young athletes off to a strong start*. NASM. https://blog.nasm.org/training-youth-athletes

Clarey, C. (2014, February 22). *Olympians use imagery as mental training*. The New York Times. https://www.nytimes.com/2014/02/23/sports/olympics/olympians-use-imagery-as-mental-training.html

Cohn, P. (n.d.). *Expectations vs. goals for athletes*. Peak Sports. https://www.peaksports.com/sports-psychology-blog/expectations-vs-goals-for-athletes/

Cohn, P. (2014a). *Sports visualization for athletes*. Peaksports.com. https://www.peaksports.com/sports-psychology-blog/sports-visualization-athletes/

Cohn, P. (2014b, December 22). *The importance of routines*. Www.peaksports.com. https://www.peaksports.com/sports-psychology-blog/the-importance-of-routines-with-olaniyi-sobomehin/

Cohn, P. (2017, April 6). *How to overcome negative thinking.* Peak Performance Sports. https://www.peaksports.com/sports-psychology-blog/how-to-overcome-negative-thinking-and-beliefs/

Cohn, P. (2021, January 28). *Build trust and confidence.* Kids' Sports Psychology. https://www.kidssportspsychology.com/help-young-athletes-build-trust-and-confidence/

Cullins, A. (2022, January 4). *7 fun goal-setting activities for children.* Big Life Journal. https://biglifejournal.com/blogs/blog/5-fun-goal-setting-activities-children

Davis, T. (2021, February 16). *Ultimate positive thinking exercises (+ 3 great techniques).* PositivePsychology.com. https://positivepsychology.com/positive-thinking-exercises/

Denys, M. (2022, April 23). *Six mistakes athletes unknowingly make: Giving power to the negative thoughts.* Seychelles Nation. https://www.nation.sc/articles/13313/six-mistakes-athletes-unknowingly-make--giving-power-to-the-negative-thoughts

Derisz, R. (2022, February 23). *You will never be successful with the wrong mindset.* Goalcast. https://www.goalcast.com/pyramid-of-success/

5 practical self-care tips for youth athletes. (2019, September 1). True Sport. https://truesport.org/preparation-recovery/5-self-care-tips-youth-athletes/

Focus meditation: How to perform focus meditation. (2022, July 22). MasterClass. https://www.masterclass.com/articles/focus-meditation

Gavin, M. (2018, February). *Why Exercise is wise (for teens).* Kidshealth.org. https://kidshealth.org/en/teens/exercise-wise.html

Gavin, M. L. (2018). *Strength training (for teens).* Kidshealth.org. https://kidshealth.org/en/teens/strength-training.html

Gleason, D. (2018, May 30). *3 tips for speed for young athletes.* Athletes Acceleration Sports Performance Training. https://athletesacceleration.com/3-tips-for-speed-for-young-athletes/

Grabowski, S. (2020, March 1). *Celebrities and athletes who meditate everyday.* THE MINDFUL STEWARD. https://themindfulsteward.

com/celebrities-and-athletes-who-meditate-everyday/

Gutierrez, S. (2015, April 15). *Developing mental toughness key to success.* Tallahassee Democrat. https://www.tallahassee.com/story/life/well ness/2015/04/20/developing-mental-toughness-key-success/ 26105115/

Guyer, B. (2022, December 10). *The ultimate guide to game day routines for athletes.* Major League Mindset. https://brandonguyer.com/ blog/the-ultimate-guide-to-game-day-routines-for-athletes

Hanford, E. (2009). *Angela Duckworth and the research on "grit".* American Public Media. http://americanradioworks.publicradio.org/ features/tomorrows-college/grit/angela-duckworth-grit.html

Hehir, J. (Director). (2020). *The Last Dance.* ESPN Studios.

Heistand, J. (2021). *5 reasons why players lose confidence in their game.* Still Point Performance. https://stillpointperformance.com/5-reasons- why-players-lose-confidence-in-their-game/

Hoff, N. (2020, October 14). *Setting positive, actionable goals.* SmartBrief. https://corp.smartbrief.com/original/2020/10/setting-positive- actionable-goals

How much physical activity do children need?. (2020, October 7). Centers for Disease Control and Prevention. https://www.cdc.gov/physi calactivity/basics/children/index.htm

How pro athletes train to get their competitive edge. (n.d. b). VertiMax. https://www.vertimax.com/blog/how-pro-athletes-train-to-get- their-competitive-edge

Hutchinson, T. S. (2022, September 8). *7 signs of mentally strong people.* Psychology Today. https://www.psychologytoday.com/us/blog/ the-pulse-mental-health/202209/7-signs-mentally-strong-people

Janssen, J. (2016). *The value of trust among coaches, athletes.* Coach and Athletic Director. https://coachad.com/articles/understanding- importance-trust/

Keim, K. (n.d.). *4 reasons every athlete should meditate.* Headspace. https:// www.headspace.com/articles/4-reasons-every-athlete-should- meditate

Leopold, B. (n.d.). *How to develop mental toughness in sports for kids.* Overcomers Counseling. https://overcomewithus.com/parenting/

how-to-develop-mental-toughness-in-sports-for-kids

Mackenzie, B. (2019). *Goal setting*. BrianMac Sports Coach. https://www.brianmac.co.uk/goals.htm

Manson, M. (2020, November 12). How to overcome your limiting beliefs. Mark Manson Blog. https://markmanson.net/limiting-beliefs#what-are-limiting-beliefs

Marcatto, F. (2018, November 28). *The five principles of effective goal-setting*. Mindiply. https://mindiply.com/blog/post/the-five-principles-of-effective-goal-setting

Mariama-Arthur, K. (2016, January 25). *Why every leader needs mental toughness*. Entrepreneur. https://www.entrepreneur.com/leadership/why-every-leader-needs-mental-toughness/250989

Mariama-Arthur, K. (2017, February 24). *Why mindset mastery is vital to your success*. Entrepreneur. https://www.entrepreneur.com/leadership/why-mindset-mastery-is-vital-to-your-success/285466

Mayo Clinic Staff. (2021, June 17). *Can you sing while you work out?* Mayo Clinic. https://www.mayoclinic.org/healthy-lifestyle/fitness/in-depth/exercise-intensity/art-20046887

Mayo Clinic Staff. (2020, April 22). *A beginner's guide to meditation*. Mayo Clinic. https://www.mayoclinic.org/tests-procedures/meditation/in-depth/meditation/art-20045858

Mead, E. (2019, June). *47 goal setting exercises, tools, & games (incl. PDF worksheets)*. PositivePsychology.com. https://positivepsychology.com/goal-setting-exercises/

Mejia, Z. (2018, February 11). 4 Olympians share what they do to achieve their goals. CNBC. https://www.cnbc.com/2018/02/11/4-olympians-share-the-mental-tips-they-use-to-achieve-their-goals.html

Milani, J. (2019, April 4). *The power of mindset on sports performance*. Sportsmd.com. https://www.sportsmd.com/2019/04/04/the-power-of-mindset-on-sports-performance/

Mindful Staff. (2020, July 8). *What is mindfulness?*. Mindful. https://www.mindful.org/what-is-mindfulness/

Morin, A. (2016, July 12). *3 reasons you should make building mental strength a top priority*. Inc.com. https://www.inc.com/amy-morin/3-

reasons-you-should-make-building-mental-strength-a-top-priority.html

Morin, A. (2018, November 27). *10 signs you're a mentally strong person (even though most people think these are weaknesses)*. Inc.com. https://www.inc.com/amy-morin/10-signs-youre-a-mentally-strong-person-even-though-most-people-think-these-are-weaknesses.html

Most disciplined football players of all time. (2021, April 21). SportMob. https://sportmob.com/en/article/963187-Most-disciplined-football-players-of-all-time

Nikitina, A. (2013, November 6). *One of the best goal setting exercises*. Lifehack. https://www.lifehack.org/articles/productivity/one-the-best-goal-setting-exercises.html

Niles, F. (2011, June 17). *How to use visualization to achieve your goals*. HuffPost. https://www.huffpost.com/entry/visualization-goals_b_878424

Nolan, D. W. (2018, January 3). *An athlete's 5 morning steps for success*. Thrive Global. https://medium.com/thrive-global/an-athletes-5-morning-steps-for-success-ee80e217240c

Pompliano, P. (2021, February 23). *7 mentally tough people on the tactics they use to build resilience*. The Profile. https://theprofile.substack.com/p/mental-toughness

Pottratz, S. (2013, May 24). Believe Perform. https://believeperform.com/overcoming-fear-of-failure-and-risk-taking/

Quashie, S. (2016, September 24). *10 of the most iconic in-game signature moves in sports*. Bleacher Report. https://bleacherreport.com/articles/2665433-10-of-the-most-iconic-in-game-signature-moves-in-sports

Quinn, E. (2011, October 4). *Positive self-talk in athletes improves performance*. Verywell Fit. https://www.verywellfit.com/positive-self-talk-3120690

Quinn, E. (2018). *Visualization and mental rehearsal can improve athletic performance*. Verywell Fit. https://www.verywellfit.com/visualization-techniques-for-athletes-3119438

Quinn, E. (2020, August 13). *Can you get stronger by just thinking about it?*

Verywell Fit. https://www.verywellfit.com/can-you-build-strength-with-visualization-exercises-3120698

Quinn, E. (2021, June 11). *How keeping a positive attitude can improve sports performance.* Verywell Fit. https://www.verywellfit.com/attitude-and-sports-performance-3974677

Razmus, A. (2020, March 11). *Building a strong mental game: the power of visualization for athletes.* Competitive Edge. https://compedgept.com/blog/visualization-and-athletic-performance/

Reaburn, P. (2018, March 27). *7 most common training mistakes by masters athletes.* Pan Pacific Masters Games. https://mastersgames.com.au/ppmg/7-most-common-training-mistakes-by-masters-athletes/

Reynolds, G. (2017, June 21). *To train an athlete, add 12 minutes of meditation to the daily mix.* The New York Times. https://www.nytimes.com/2017/06/21/well/live/to-train-an-athlete-add-12-minutes-of-meditation-to-the-daily-mix.html

Rhodes, J. (2021, July 12). *The top 25 mentoring movies of all time!* The Chronicle of Evidence Based Monitoring. https://www.evidencebasedmentoring.org/top-25-mentoring-relationships-represented-in-film/

Robbins, T. (2017, February 9). *6 strategic tips to reprogram your mind.* Tonyrobbins.com. https://www.tonyrobbins.com/mind-meaning/how-to-reprogram-your-mind/

Scott, E. (2021, April 25). *Do you have FOMO? Here is how to cope.* Verywell Mind. https://www.verywellmind.com/how-to-cope-with-fomo-4174664

Scott, E. (2022, December 1). *Can mindfulness relieve more than stress?* Verywell Mind. https://www.verywellmind.com/mindfulness-the-health-and-stress-relief-benefits-3145189#toc-impact-of-mindfulness

7 things mentally strong people don't waste time doing, according to a psychotherapist. (2020, January 19). Business Insider. https://www.businessinsider.in/slideshows/miscellaneous/7-things-mentally-strong-people-dont-waste-time-doing-according-to-a-psychotherapist/slidelist/73387594.cms#slideid=73387610

Sherwood, A. (2018, January 26). *What is positive thinking?* WebMD.

https://www.webmd.com/mental-health/positive-thinking-overview

Sigl, C. (n.d.). *Overcoming perfectionism in youth sports*. Mental Toughness Trainer. https://www.mentaltoughnesstrainer.com/overcoming-perfectionism/

Star, K. (2018). *Mindfulness meditation exercise for anxiety*. Verywell Mind. https://www.verywellmind.com/mindfulness-meditation-exercise-for-anxiety-2584081

Straw, E. (2022a, December 28). *Top 10 costly mental game mistakes athletes make*. Success Starts Within. https://www.successstartswithin.com/blog/top-10-costly-mental-game-mistakes

Straw, E. (2022b, December 28). *Visualization techniques for athletes-success starts within*. Success Starts Within. https://www.successstartswithin.com/blog/visualization-techniques-for-athletes

Strong, B. (2016, September 14). *21 signs you're mentally stronger than average*. Business Insider. https://www.businessinsider.in/strategy/21-signs-youre-mentally-stronger-than-average/articleshow/54330069.cms

Suchde, S. (2013, October 23). *A professional athlete's fitness regime: An insider's guide*. The Health Site. https://www.thehealthsite.com/fitness/a-professional-athletes-fitness-regime-an-insiders-guide-88398/

Swaim, E. (2022, March 9). *Why sports anxiety happens and how to cope*. Healthline. https://www.healthline.com/health/sports-performance-anxiety

Swenson, C. (2021, March 8). *The rule of thirds*. Connor Swenson Blog. https://www.connorswenson.com/blog/rule-of-thirds

Taylor, J. (2012, July 17). *Sports: Why the world's best athletes use routines*. Psychology Today. https://www.psychologytoday.com/us/blog/the-power-prime/201207/sports-why-the-worlds-best-athletes-use-routines

Taylor, J. (2014, November 12). *3 essential mindsets for athletic success*. Psychology Today. https://www.psychologytoday.com/us/blog/the-power-prime/201411/3-essential-mindsets-athletic-success

The 8 best strength exercises for youth athletes. (n.d.). Dynamic Strength and Training. Retrieved February 17, 2023, from https://www. dynamicsc.com/blog/the-8-best-strength-exercises-for-youth-athletes

The best athletic & sports affirmations for performance. (n.d.). SelfPause. https://selfpause.com/affirmations/athletic-affirmations/

3 ways young athletes can improve stamina and endurance. (2016, December 27). Rocky Top Sports World. https://rockytopsports world.com/blog/how-young-athletes-can-improve-stamina-and-endurance/

Time management for young athletes. (2018). US Youth Soccer. https:// www.usyouthsoccer.org/news/ time_management_for_young_athletes/

Warm-up routine: A guide for high school athletes. (2020, November 17). MTS Physical Therapy and Wellness. http://www.mtsphysicalther apy.com/news/warm-up-routine-a-guide-for-high-school-athletes

Waehner, P. (2021, March 30). *10 things to stop doing if you want to start exercising.* Verywell Fit. https://www.verywellfit.com/things-to-stop-if-you-want-to-exercise-1231403

Wensor, D. (2017, March 2). *6 tips for best competition preparation.* Coaching Young Athletes. https://coachingyoungathletes.com/ 2017/03/02/6-tips-for-best-competition-preparation/

What is mental toughness?. (n.d.). Mental Toughness Inc. https://www. mentaltoughnessinc.com/what-is-mental-toughness/

Why mental toughness is critically important?. (2020). Mental Toughness Partners. https://www.mentaltoughness.partners/why-mental-toughness-is-critically-important/

Whyte, E. (2019, January 15). *The importance of goal setting for athletes.* Metrifit Athlete Monitoring and Well-Being. https://metrifit.com/ blog/the-importance-of-goal-setting-for-athletes/

Wilson, L. (2019, March 4). *Positive self-talk for your athletes.* Coaches Toolbox. https://www.coachestoolbox.net/mental-toughness/posi tive-self-talk-for-your-athletes

Wolfe, A., & Lastoe, S. (2020, June 19). *10 Olympic athletes' daily habits to inspire you.* The Muse. https://www.themuse.com/advice/10-

olympic-athletes-daily-habits-you-should-steal-that-dont-involve-the-gym

York Morris, S. (2016, July 12). What are the benefits of self-talk? Healthline; Healthline Media. https://www.healthline.com/health/mental-health/self-talk

IMAGE REFERENCES

Borja Blanco Cinza. (2020, May 7). [Image]. Pixabay. https://pixabay.com/vectors/meditation-yoga-relaxation-zen-5138375/

Clker–Free–Vektor–Images. (2012, April 18). Baseball Batter. [Image]. Pixabay.   https://pixabay.com/vectors/baseball-player-batter-hitting-37703/

Clker–Free–Vektor–Images. (2014, August 1). Defense Guard. [Image]. Pixabay.   https://pixabay.com/vectors/defense-guard-basketball-athlete-311598/

Everesd_desgin. (2020, mAY 25). Medals. [Image]. Pixabay. https://pixabay.com/vectors/medals-winner-medal-victory-master-5213756/

Gerd Altmann. (2022, July 22). Mental Resilience. [Image]. Pixabay. https://pixabay.com/illustrations/mental-health-resilience-protection-7337256/

Maki. (2016, March 31). Destination. [Image]. Pixabay. https://pixabay.com/vectors/destination-goal-purpose-the-goal-1285851/

Megan Rexazin. (2019, September 22). Time Management. [Image]. Pixabay.   https://pixabay.com/vectors/clock-time-management-time-4496464/

Mohamed Hassan. (2021, August 22). Fear Anxiety. [Image]. Pixabay. https://pixabay.com/vectors/fear-anxiety-depression-woman-6562668/

Mohamed Hassan. (2018, August 2). Martial Arts. [Image]. Pixabay. https://pixabay.com/vectors/silhouette-kung-fu-wushu-shaolin-3577338/

Mohamed Hassan. (2013, February 9). Mindset. [Image]. Pixabay.

https://pixabay.com/vectors/mindset-personality-mental-health-7777233/

Mohamed Hassan. (2021, November 7). Support Help. [Image]. Pixabay. https://pixabay.com/vectors/support-help-mountain-climbing-6773819/

Mohamed Hassan. (2018, September 15). Track. [Image]. Pixabay. https://pixabay.com/illustrations/sport-athlete-track-runner-field-3677470/

Mohamed Hassan. (2019, January 22). Weightlifting. [Image]. Pixabay. https://pixabay.com/vectors/weightlifter-gym-tool-athlete-3944725/

Mohamed Hassan. (2019, May 7). Woman Run. [Image]. Pixabay. https://pixabay.com/vectors/woman-run-treadmill-silhouette-4183803/

Mohamed Hassan. (2022, June 8). Yoga Practice. [Image]. Pixabay. https://pixabay.com/vectors/yoga-training-meditation-relaxation-7249207/

OpenClipart–Vectors. (2016, April 1). Athletic Basketball. [Image]. Pixabay. https://pixabay.com/vectors/athlete-athletic-ball-basketball-1299436/

OpenClipart–Vectors. (2013, October 11). Handball. [Image]. Pixabay. https://pixabay.com/vectors/handball-basketball-ball-people-150163/

OpenClipart–Vectors. (2013, October 13). High Jump. [Image]. Pixabay. https://pixabay.com/vectors/high-jump-olympics-high-150517/

OpenClipart–Vectors. (2017, January 31). Podium. [Image]. Pixabay. https://pixabay.com/vectors/podium-rostrum-victor-victory-win-2026694/

OpenClipart–Vectors. (2013, October 13). Sports Athletics. [Image]. Pixabay. https://pixabay.com/vectors/sports-athletics-collage-baseball-150518/

Made in United States
Troutdale, OR
10/02/2023

13361231R00110